# BUILDING
# LONDON

## The making of a modern metropolis

### BRUCE MARSHALL

MAINSTREAM
PUBLISHING

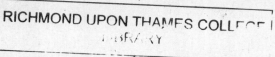
First published in Great Britain in 2007 by
MAINSTREAM PUBLISHING COMPANY
(EDINBURGH) LTD
7 Albany Street
Edinburgh EH1 3UG

This book was produced by
Endeavour London Ltd
21–31 Woodfield Road
London W9 2BA
Fax 44 (0) 20 7579 5710
info@EndeavourLondon.com

Managing Editor: Mark Fletcher
Proofreader: Liz Ihre
Picture Research: Ali Khoja
Design: Paul Welti
Production: Mary Osborne

Printed in China

# Contents

# Introduction

London is a frustrating place. On the one hand it can be beautiful, ancient and atmospheric, and then it can be simply ugly and grimly nondescript. One loves London in the same way that one loves a relative; you don't necessarily always like them. Helping to present BBC TV's *Restoration* programme, I am regularly reminded of such family feelings, as buildings stimulate, cry out for TLC, or are best ignored.

Fundamentally, London suffers from its featureless and underlying estuarine topography. The clay beneath it yielded the somewhat unappealing muddy brown stock bricks which made its houses, and any building stone had to be imported. It's not like Edinburgh where hill-topping fine stone buildings crown views and vistas. And yet from this unprepossessing and marshy site rose a fabulous city that capitalised on the one natural feature of true distinction, the River Thames. With its wide curves and strange double backs, this river appears and reappears throughout the city, and its great width gives London vistas of a different character to Paris and the Seine. The great medieval builders understood this when they created their city of church towers all over sailed by the tall central spire of

St Paul's Cathedral. All this was lost in the Great Fire of 1666, but was rebuilt, miraculously, even more elegantly and crisply in Portland stone by Sir Christopher Wren and his collaborators. This was the composition painted by Canaletto and was, perhaps, the finest skyline of any city in Europe.

Now we are encouraged to admire the exciting muddle of new high rise blocks in the City. But London is not New York, and the scale is wrong and the overall sense of composition has been lost. While New York can be seen from across the broad East River, London now overcrowds the Thames. Stand now on any river bridge and see how the scattering of tall blocks along the river has destroyed the physical focus that London once had. Only the distant cluster of Canary Wharf conveys some sense of composition. New buildings rise up unexpectedly here and there, like weeds in a lawn, sometimes dramatic and bold, but more often they are intrusive and discourteous. Rather like modern Tokyo, what is uniform is now merely the visual chaos that is spreading up and down the river, mile after mile. While Christopher Wren consciously sought to glorify the city as a single entity, these new buildings seek to dissolve its boundaries, adding new prominence to random locations simply to inflate the profits of their developers and the reputations of their designers.

Bruce Marshall's *Building London* reveals quickly just how dramatic this process of change has been over the last over hundred and fifty years. There's the clean Victorian streetscape that was Holborn Circus at the turn of the twentieth century, before the awful clutter of modern street signs, lights and congestion charge security cameras. And Old London Bridge with its elegant granite arches, now sacrificed in the name of traffic flow. For the last fifty years we have had greater planning controls than ever before, but it is ironic that over this time the overall appearance of London has probably changed more than ever before.

But for all the change, the images in this book also reinforce how visually rich and stimulating London remains. Street after street is crafted with care and detail, each building forming the backdrop to the everyday lives and activity of its citizens. There is an enriched modesty in the ordinary townscape that we all take for granted, where the craftsmanship of construction was celebrated but without usurping the value of the whole. We must cherish and protect what we have, however unfashionable it may be, in the knowledge that London will always go on changing and relentlessly re-developing itself in different ways long after we have gone.

PTOLEMY DEAN

The pilings for Lambeth's river wall take root in the 1860s. This was church land where, for centuries, the Archbishop of Canterbury's fine palace had overlooked struggling development of a swampy tract. Now the long process of civilizing the South Bank could begin.

# Prologue

A river and worlds apart: the fragile Globe Theatre in sinful Southwark on the neglected southern side of the Thames, and the White Tower at the heart of the Tower of London on its northern bank – a formidable statement of the City's permanence and precedence.

Around AD 40, Roman warships probed the English Channel's northern shoreline and found the Thames Estuary. Fifty miles upriver there were the right conditions for a base camp in a natural amphitheatre – the London Basin – formed by low hills. To the south there was an intermittent crescent of them from Greenwich round to Richmond; to the north Ludgate Hill and Cornhill, with Hampstead, more than 400 ft. high, far beyond. The river, though wider than it is today, could be bridged here, perhaps even forded, and its size indicated that it went deep into the hinterland.

The Romans built a city wall, started a thriving port, erected public buildings – a forum, a basilica, an amphitheatre, baths – typical of all their colonies. All these sank below the surface after their departure in the fifth century, since the Germanic tribes that replaced them were not city types. But six centuries later William the Conqueror put down a marker that lasts to this day: the White Tower at the heart of the Tower of London, a stern stone statement that the Normans were here to stay. Medieval London grew around it, soon bursting out beyond the remaining scraps of the Roman walls.

Builders did not have far to look for materials. There were rushes for thatching at the river's edges, and oak aplenty for framing and fuel – the forest spread northward as far as the eye could see. The London Basin provided chalk and gravel, beds of pebbles in Blackheath and Woolwich, and belts of sands. And there was clay for the red and the yellow "London stock" bricks that would become the signature material in deposits that were 400 ft. deep. Much later, when the Victorians were making it the world's largest city – its population larger than those of Paris, Berlin, Vienna, and St Petersburg combined in 1901 – the night sky seemed to be supported on the fiery glow of the brick kilns.

London was not clearly the capital until the 14th century: Winchester, York, and Oxford also had claims for that position. But London had a port generating prosperity, a honeypot for successive monarchs who devised ever more ingenious taxes on it, and when the King's courts of law were set up it was at Westminster, a short boat-ride up the river. There was also a concentration of Church power and property in London – monasteries, friaries, nunneries, schools, churches, and abbeys, plus a monopoly hold on profitable services such as ferry crossings. With State and Church ensconced, growth was explosive, but it was unplanned and socially divisive. The merchant classes stayed where they were in what became the "City", cranking the money machine around St Paul's and their headquarters at the Guildhall, but the lawyers, nobility and those with social aspirations started to move steadily westwards into the prevailing wind, which could then carry away the smoke of countless coal fires. Theirs was the West End, down the Strand, then in due course along Piccadilly to Hyde Park, before eventually burgeoning out to Belgravia, Chelsea, Knightsbridge, and Kensington. The wind also blew away the smell of the "stink industries" fuelled by the port and by the labour of the poor huddled in the East End, the far side of the City.

As to the area south of the river, its development took longer and, indeed, never generated the grand and gracious characteristics of the other bank. The Romans had made a road to a junction at Elephant and Castle, where their legions could turn right for Winchester, or left for Dover and

TOWER OF LONDON. THE WHITE TOWER. 8.62. L.S.&P.C°.        STEREOSCOPIC C° L™.

Canterbury. This was the road that Chaucer and his pilgrims took from London and its traffic also included Canterbury's Archbishops, whose eye for real estate was astute. The Church acquired much of south London – indeed the Archbishop built his London residence at Lambeth and the Bishops of Winchester and Rochester theirs at Southwark. In later times those landholdings would benefit south London communities: when space was desperately needed for suburban growth and the railways to serve it, the Church proved to be a less greedy freeholder than the aristocrats who owned the great estates north of the river.

In the 16th century there was an increasing tendency for the royal court to stay in and around London, hence Henry VIII's building activities at Whitehall, St James's, Bridewell, Greenwich and elsewhere. This was also the period when the Inns of Court, where the lawyers lived communally either side of the western

The Venetian-style bridge at the mouth of the Fleet gives a misleading impression of that river's vitality. By the time Samuel Scott painted this romanticised view, in about 1750, the clear waters that flowed down from the heights of Hampstead were the city's main sewage carrier. A few years later, this last stretch to the Thames was channelled underground.

boundary of the City at Temple Bar, came to prominence. It was their members who provided much of the sophisticated audience for the new theatres on the South Bank. These were the sorts of influences which drove the population up from 75,000 in 1500 to 250,000 in 1600. Two great gifts were bestowed on London in the 17th century by the architect Inigo Jones and his followers, who looked to Italy for inspiration: the classical style of building and the species of town planning known as the square. They functioned together by means of the terrace, in which façades follow a common design enabling a large architectural gesture to be made out of a number of individual dwellings. Wren, Hawksmoor, Gibbs, Adam, Chambers, and Soane continued the good work into the 18th century and beyond, helped both by the opportunities that opened up after the Fire of London in 1666, and by gifted amateurs like Lord Burlington. Nash provided the final flourish round Regent's Park, and down Regent Street to the Mall.

The Victorian builders had much to do, providing for a population that almost reached 7 million by 1900. (A great turning point had come in 1790 when, for the first time, London's birth rate exceeded its death rate.) This was the age of monster museums and railway stations, of the new Houses of Parliament and many new churches, of the proliferation of bridges, of department stores, theatres, and music halls, of a rash of schools made necessary by the 1870 education act, and blocks of mansion flats going upwards while long ribbons of terraced housing spread outwards wherever the trains went. When it came to style, they were spoilt for choice, but often plumped for Gothic. This was also the time when the city's gleaming Portland stone and stucco facings turned black in the coal-fired smog – the "pea-soupers" through which Sherlock Holmes dramatically emerged from time to time. Dark-red and terracotta bricks were used to pre-empt discolouration, and even shiny glazed ones to help the rain wash away the grime.

The first attempt at a governing body, the Metropolitan Board of Works, embanked the river, provided a desperately needed sewerage system and oversaw the first Underground lines. But it was not until the advent of the London County Council that young planners and architects were employed, who were motivated by the Fabian vision of what the 20th century should be: that the workers had a right to bathrooms and patches of lawn. Norman Shaw and Edward Lutyens fulfilled the grand private and commercial commissions while the LCC architects provided public housing and community facilities.

The 1940–41 Blitz hit the East End, the Docks, and Lambeth hardest as well as destroying the House of Commons, many of the City livery company halls and much of the Inns of Court. Then the post-war generation of planners, however public-spirited, sometimes seemed to be compounding the war damage: Londoners marooned in the high-rise apartment blocks that arose on bomb sites yearned for the neighbourly terraces of their upbringing, while traffic engineers did their worst in the surrounding streets. Indeed, architecture disappointed at every level, with multi-storey car parks seeming the most noticeable new buildings. For some time the restoration and preservation of areas like Covent Garden, Spitalfields, Islington, Fitzrovia, or Notting Hill were the most encouraging signs, rather than anything new.

But cities are durable monsters, and thankfully the venerable old City once again lifted up its skirts and made the running. Wealth created by the "Big Bang" deregulation of financial services spilled into building there, out to Docklands, and into the transport infrastructure. Fine architects who had demonstrated their skills in Paris, Hong Kong, and New York returned to exciting commissions, like the Lloyd's Building for Richard Rogers, or the Millennium Bridge and the Gherkin for Norman Foster. Nicholas Grimshaw built a swerving caterpillar of a terminus for the Eurostar trains at Waterloo and the stations on the Tube's new Jubilee Line are full of invention and imagination. "Light and bright" joined the vocabulary in the high-tech, boomtown renaissance. London Pride was on the way back.

Another attempt to give south London a greater share of the city's action, City Hall (left) anchors the More London development near Tower Bridge. Its unlikely form demonstrates the prowess of a new force in the construction industry – structural engineers, in this case Arup. A forgotten *tour de force* by an earlier engineer, an iron bridge by Isambard Kingdom Brunel, was discovered hidden under a later road bridge being demolished at the new Paddington Basin complex (below). It is to be re-erected as a footbridge over the Grand Union Canal.

# Fit for a King

## ROYAL PALACES

(Opposite) Tourists' carriages and cabs line up outside the Tower of London in 1858, a decade after its walls were strengthened for the last time, by command of its Constable, the Duke of Wellington. The duke's fear had been civil unrest and mob attack.

The frontage of Buckingham Palace (below) is three times as wide as the original house .

There was consternation at Court about the new neighbour's plans. Across from th modest redbrick palace of St James's, a grand new house was going up, ostentatious placed to suggest that the royal park stretching to Whitehall was its front garden. Fc the moment, all the Court do could do was ban the Duke of Buckingham from maki showy approaches to his home along the royal carriageways. A little more than 50 ye later, in 1762, George III bought Buckingham House. It would become Buckingham Pa

Upstaging the neighbours had previously been the sovereign's prerogative, fir demonstrated on Tower Hill, where William the Conqueror built a square, Caen-st citadel to impress upon the locals that the Norman Conquest was here to stay. By Edward I's time, the property had expanded to 18 walled acres that would serve a palace, mint, armoury, menagerie, safe haven for the Crown Jewels, prison and tort chamber for high-profile enemies of the state, and starting point for the royal proc sions so beloved of Londoners.

There was also the Palace of Westminster where kings and parliaments spen centuries in uneasy dialogue. Its principal building, Westminster Hall, built by Willian Conqueror's son, William Rufus, was and remains the largest Norman hall in the co try. The earliest parliaments met here; citizens came to it seeking justice at the king courts of law. Occasionally it was the venue for coronation banquets. When St Stephen's Chapel, gilded, painted, and richly ornamented, was secularized in 1548, it internal configuration — choir stalls facing each other, an altar that made way for a Speaker's chair — created a natural debating chamber. The Mother of Parliaments sa here until the fire of 1834.

The Palace of Westminster was too sombre an ambience for Henry VIII. He had his eye on York House, the extravagant, sophisticated home of

Could a family retreat ever look like a palace? This work, in 1913, was the sixth and last attempt to give Buckingham Palace a regal presence – a Portland stone refacing in the Beaux-Arts style.

the endangered Archbishop of York, Cardinal Wolsey. His dismissal allowed Henry to create his palace at Whitehall, one that became "truly royal: enclosed on one side by the Thames, on the other by a park…. Near the palace are a great number of swans, who wander up and down the river for some miles in great security."

In fact, the proximity of that admired water had its downside. There are records of banquets at Whitehall Palace being disrupted as high tides flooded the kitchens. William III was convinced that the dampness aggravated his asthma; his wife tired of

State apartments at Buckingham Palace owe much of their magnificence to the Prince Regent's tastes. As George IV, he transferred many of his Carlton House treasures here to set its themes and styles. "Chippendale" chairs in the Indian Room (second down, right) are carved from ivory; the swords and daggers are from Edward VII's collection. The Chinese Room (third down) acquired its furnishings from the Regent's Brighton Pavilion. One of the massive mirrors in the most richly gilded apartment, the White Drawing Room (bottom), swings open for dramatic royal entrances.

Cardinal Wolsey entertained at his Hampton Court Palace (right) "to the wonderment of all of Europe," before forfeiting it to Henry VIII. Henry was the first of many monarchs to consider this finest example of Tudor architecture their favourite palace, and to spend extravagantly, and usually stylishly, on it; Inigo Jones, Wren, Kent, Vanbrugh, Grinling Gibbons all contributed. Just a barge ride along the Thames from Westminster, it offered peace and privacy among woods, gardens, and deer parks. Drake and Raleigh brought exotic plants from their travels to please Elizabeth I. "Capability" Brown planted the Great Vine, now thought to be the oldest in the world. Mythical heraldic beasts line the bridge over the moat. Henry VIII commissioned the Astronomical Clock (above and left) which tells hours, days, weeks, months, years.

looking at water and walls. They escaped to a "country" home on higher ground on the far side of "an impassable gulf of mud," where Wren and Hawksmoor reconstructed the Earl of Nottingham's house as Kensington Palace.

Henry married twice at Whitehall Palace, and died there. It came to have 2,000 rooms, with galleries and courts, halls for masques, a chapel, tennis court, cockpit and banqueting hall. In one of the many fires that seared the complex, the banqueting hall was razed (1619), allowing Inigo Jones to build the Palladian masterpiece that remains to this day. It took three years to build and cost £14,940.

The fire that laid waste to most of Royal Whitehall, in 1689, brought into use St James's Palace, another of Henry's acquisitions, a gloomy manor that had replaced a hospital founded for "maidens that were leprous." Foreign ambassadors are still formally accredited to the Court of St James.

A later prince proved to be the most extravagant of all royal home-makers. George III's eldest son, who was to become Prince Regent, spent 30 years renovating Carlton House on Pall Mall to the degree that it became "a palace to rank with Versailles." His architect, Henry Holland, imported columns of Sienna marble; agents were despatched to China to find furniture. In 1814 John Nash designed new buildings in the gardens solely to house 2,000 guests at a celebration for the Duke of Wellington.

When the Prince Regent became George IV, even this splendid statement did not match his perception of the sovereign's status. Nearby was the magnificently-sited Buckingham House. It should be demolished and a palace constructed in its place. The government balked at that, authorising less than half the budget the King sought. So the project became one of disguise and display which Nash, now the favoured architect, was encouraged to interpret as meaning new wings, facings of Bath stone, and vast quantities of Italian marble. George IV did not live to see the work finished, nor the final bills, for three times the authorised expenditure.

By the time Queen Victoria moved in (she was told of her accession at Kensington Palace, her mother's home) much repair and improvement were necessary. Nash's approach had been more visionary than practical; workmanship and plumbing were not befitting a royal palace. Later architects, Edward Blore and Sir Aston Webb, made further efforts to give this "country" house an Imperial air. Blore's new frontage (1847) required the removal of Nash's grand gateway, the Marble Arch, which now looms over a scruffy traffic island at the north-east corner of Hyde Park.

Despite fires and rebuildings, St James's Palace, the oldest building in the royal enclave, still has a strong castellated and towered red-brick Tudor presence around four central courtyards. Every sovereign from Henry VIII to Queen Victoria resided here at some point in their lives; it is where Elizabeth II made her first speech as Queen, in 1952.

ST JAMES'S · PALACE.

Across the road from the debating chambers, Portcullis House provides new offices for parliamentarians. The anachronistic-looking chimneys do indeed have a job to do, as part of a low-energy ventilation system.
MICHAEL HOPKINS & PARTNERS, 2000

# The mother of all parliaments

## THE HOUSES OF PARLIAMENT

A fire set to burn old tax records – centuries' worth of notched elmwood sticks – in a furnace under the House of Lords flared out of control, destroying the Palace of Westminster in 1834. The good news was the opportunity it afforded for the two Houses of Parliament to accommodate themselves in a building specifically designed for their use.

Almost 100 architects entered the design competition, with the brief "Gothic or Elizabethan" pinned to their drawing boards (somehow, over the centuries, Gothic had become identified by the British as a style of their own devising). Fortunately, late or Tudor Gothic won; or Westminster might by now have the air of a theme park. The winning architect, was the accomplished but eclectic Sir Charles Barry, just as much at home working in a Renaissance or an Italianate style. His assistant, Augustus Welby Northmore Pugin, was, however, the leading advocate of true archaeologically-based, Gothic architecture, and himself the son of a French-born Gothic expert. Barry's symmetrical Thames frontage combined with the completely asymmetrical skyline, with its two constrasting towers and a fleche, is witness to his eclecticism. Much of the Perpendicular detailing and all the furnishings are Pugin's.

The Lords moved in in 1847, the Commons four years later. The new palace at

Westminster was considered a wonder of the age... "one of the most magnificent buildings ever erected continuously in Europe – the largest modern Gothic edifice in the world." The Royal, or Victoria, Tower did not reach its full height of 340 feet for some years: concerned about settlement in the riverside mud, the builders tentatively added 30 ft. of stonework a year. Completed, safely, in 1860, it was then hailed as "one of the most stupendous works of its kind ever conceived".

Queen Victoria's Consort, Prince Albert, had a hand in the interior decoration, encouraging "much magnificence" by way, for example, of huge frescoes from the legend of King Arthur, Venetian mosaics, and statues of Magna Carta barons. In all, this "vast and splendid" building cost £3 million.

Installing Big Ben – properly, that is the name of just the bell – behind the Pugin-designed clockfaces (above right) was one of the more fraught projects at the Palace. The first casting was an unsuitable mix of copper and tin, and cracked, as did the second, when an overweight clapper hammer was fitted. Nevertheless the great clock met its specification – to be accurate to within a second a day.

Twenty years after the Palace's foundation stone was laid in 1837, the Victoria Tower, the most problematic feature for the builders, nears completion. The Big Ben Tower is still under scaffolding. Westminster Abbey is in the left background.

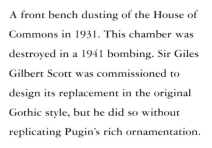

A front bench dusting of the House of Commons in 1931. This chamber was destroyed in a 1941 bombing. Sir Giles Gilbert Scott was commissioned to design its replacement in the original Gothic style, but he did so without replicating Pugin's rich ornamentation.

# Corridors of power

## GOVERNMENT BUILDINGS

Whitehall is a thoroughfare, a precinct with a purpose, and a synonym for a frame of mind. The purpose is government; the frame of mind is bureaucratic. For several centuries now, architects have tried to express the power of the first while floundering in the indecisiveness of the second. Wren had a grand plan for Whitehall, so did Sir John Soane. They came to nothing. After World War II more than one modern masterplan was widely applauded, then discarded. Whitehall, the nation's administrative heart, remains, like so much of London, a medley of styles and vintages.

After the burning of Whitehall Palace, where the monarch conducted the affairs of state amid the diversionary politicking of courtiers and courtesans, the Court moved on to St James's Palace – geographically on the fringe, and, as the constitutional monarchy adopted its modern form, symbolically so. The political establishment and the burgeoning bureaucracy at first adapted fine private houses for their purposes, most notably in the case of the prime minister's official residence. There is no White House or Elysée Palace or Kremlin in Whitehall. The electorate's choice of leader lives and works

Amid Whitehall's more daunting power statements, the Horse Guards has the comforting appeal of rusticated masonry and modest arches. Once a year, the parade ground fills with colour for the celebration of the sovereign's official birthday, the Trooping of the Colour.
**WILLIAM KENT, WILLIAM ROBINSON, JOHN VARDEY, 1755**

The Ministry of Defence, a massive complex seen from the side which overlooks the river. During its construction, Henry VIII's wine cellar was unearthed. It has been preserved.

VINCENT HARRIS, 1959

HOME OFFICE, 1873

OLD WAR OFFICE, 1906

TREASURY BUILDING, 1844

MINISTRY OF DEFENCE, 1949 (COMPLETED 1959)

FOREIGN AND COMMONWEALTH OFFICE, 1875

## POSITIONS OF POWER, OUTPOSTS OF EMPIRE

As the Whitehall bureaucracy grew, converted townhouses and modestly elegant quarters created by William Kent and Sir John Soane made way for Victorian power blocks, with Sir George Gilbert Scott and Sir Charles Barry as favoured architects. High Commissioners, the Empire's diplomatic representatives, vied to acquire corner sites along the Strand and Aldwych to position themselves prominently close to the centre of government. Rhodesia, later Zimbabwe, took over a building by Charles Holden. Then, with Australia House (1918), A.M. and A.G.R. Mackenzie set a style for Imperial government buildings, to be followed by Sir Herbert Baker's India House (1930) and South Africa House in Trafalgar Square (1933). The structures were London-stately; the interiors were often notable for indigenous materials and motifs.

(Opposite) Wreaths at the foot of the Cenotaph in Whitehall after a Remembrance Day service. The lines of the Portland Stone pier are all slightly curved, indicating infinity. There are no religious symbols.
SIR EDWARD LUTYENS, 1920

SOUTH AFRICA HOUSE, 1933

INDIA HOUSE, 1930

RHODESIA HOUSE (NOW ZIMBABWE HOUSE), 1908

AUSTRALIA HOUSE, 1918

behind a modest, terrace-house frontage in Downing Street, as have prime ministers since 1735. The appearance, though, is deceptive: No.10 incorporates a much larger house behind, overlooking Horse Guards Parade. (Indeed, Nos 10 and 11 – the Chancellor of the Exchequer's quarters – are presently valued at £23 million in the national property portfolio.)

The first purpose-built government buildings had this dual role – official residence, seat of power. S.P. Cockerell's Admiralty House (1788) was one such. Then, the importance of the department could be deduced from the grandeur of its housing, as in William Kent's Treasury Block (1734) with its extravagantly-detailed meeting rooms. Fine architects were at work, and powerful men with idiosyncratic tastes were signing-off on the bills. Thus in the Whitehall precinct, Neo-Baroque

The title on the door of No. 10 – "First Lord of the Treasury" pre-dates "prime minister" as the designation of the leader of government – can no longer be admired by casual visitors who must now view Downing Street through security gates.

stands alongside High Victorian Gothic, French Second Empire meets Palladian. Occasionally the Treasury put its foot down. Sir George Gilbert Scott's Home Office and Colonial Office building of the 1870s never got the tall towers he had intended for each corner.

The Victorians pulled down distinguished Soane buildings to put up power piles, and construction crews have been busy ever since, mostly adapting and refurbishing as government departments, becoming more or less crucial to the nation's well-being, have moved quarters. The one truly new building is Portcullis House (2000), a stone and bronze complex of offices for parliamentarians, across the road from the House of Commons, connected to it by a subway.

"The finest group of buildings which London possesses."
*THE ENCYCLOPEDIA BRITANNICA (1911)*

# Where the law stands

## INNS AND COURTS

Behind the massive doors of the Gatehouse at Lincoln's Inn is a picturesque precinct of brick houses, courtyards, halls, and a chapel. The Old Hall dates from 1492, the Gatehouse from 1518.

Litigation was a lively London practice as early as the 14th century. And like other professionals who would later congregate in distinct neighbourhoods — jewellers in Hatton Garden, tailors in Savile Row — lawyers founded a colony, on a salubrious swathe of land, neutrally and conveniently between the City and Westminster. What began haphazardly as hostels for like legal minds became residential colleges with all the campus graces of Oxford and Cambridge. The four Inns of Court were "the noblest nurseries of Humanity and Liberty in the Kingdom," said Ben Jonson.

By Elizabethan times, 2,000 students at a time were being trained by their elders at the Inns. (At that time, the word "inn" defined a wealthy household.) The most northerly was Gray's Inn, the biggest and most prestigious in the 16th century. To the south, across High Holborn, is Lincoln's Inn; then the Middle and Inner Temples, with gardens down to the Thames, separated from it now by the Victoria Embankment.

At the heart of each Inn is a Great Hall where students are obliged to dine regularly before being called to the Bar — that is, to qualify as barristers. Lawyers'

Middle Temple Hall is considered the finest remaining Elizabethan building in London. There was a famous performance by Shakespeare's company of *Twelfth Night* here in 1602. Queen Elizabeth donated the timber for one of its dining tables – three 30-ft. planks from a single Windsor Forest oak tree.

One of the great London street survivals – the half-timbered façade of Staple Inn in Holborn, built in the 1580s, and much renovated since. Staple Inn was an Inn of Chancery, out-ranked by the Inns of Court. It was linked with Gray's Inn.

offices – chambers – stand in orderly rows or, particularly in the Temples, crowded around picturesque passageways. There is building from every period of English architecture, some of it restorative replication after the Inns suffered severe beatings in World War II bombings.

And nearby, the barristers practise their skills at the Royal Courts of Justice, across the road from the entrances to the Temples. This is the location for civil cases that were formerly heard in Westminster Hall. The architect was the church builder George Edward Street, and there is, indeed, a cathedral-like air to this intricately detailed Gothic Revival complex of 1,000 rooms. Queen Victoria opened the building in 1882.

Serious criminal cases were traditionally tried at the Sessions House in Old Bailey, some distance to the east of legal London. The Central Criminal Court built there in 1907 is crowned by a dome and a 12-ft. high gilded figure of Justice, a symbol almost as well known as the Statue of Liberty. It is a stern building, but not as grim as the notorious Newgate Prison that previously occupied the site.

Charles Dickens, who worked there briefly as a clerk, was not greatly taken with Gray's Inn (far left above) – "can anything be more dreary than its arid square?" He had more sympathy with the concepts of Truth and Justice, seated beside the Recording Angel over the entrance to the Old Bailey (left above).

Inside and out, the Royal Courts of Justice display meticulous craftsmanship. Around the base of the building, a frieze depicting artisans at work is the architect's tribute to his team. In front of the clock tower, a bronze dragon on a plinth marks the boundary of the City of London. It replaced Temple Bar (above), removed in 1878 to ease traffic flow.

An 18th-century engraving of a 13th-century extravagance at Westminster Abbey – a pavement of porphyry and marble, the pieces brought from Rome along with the craftsmen who knew how to assemble them. The abbot who commissioned the work is thought to be buried under the oblong.

The most French-looking of all English cathedrals, Westminster Abbey is yet the heart of the English church/state establishment, the place where monarchs are crowned and many are buried, and the edifice that dominates Parliament Square, the centre of government. Fragments of Edward the Confessor's 11th-century abbey remain, but the church of today is largely the one begun 200 years later. Devotion to its care is in part due to its status as the national shrine, filled with monuments and statuary of the great, most richly in Poets' Corner (right).

# Pride and prayer

## PLACES OF WORSHIP

Church and state were inseparably bonded in early London. The units of local government were the parishes – a parish being a church district. The 12th century City had 120 churches serving and controlling an average of 300 parishioners each. At state level, the bond was as firm: Westminster Abbey and the royal Palace of Westminster grew side by side, in the same complex. Civil servants were clerics.

And religion was a profit centre. It was customary for a third of a wealthy estate to be left to the Church, for which chantry priests sang masses for the souls of the benefactors. Pews were rented out to families, confessions, burials and weddings handled at a price. The smarter the building, the higher the steeple, the louder the bells rang out, the more passing trade could be attracted, against competition from the monastic orders whose more obvious saintliness earned them rich bequests and endowments. At the time of Henry VIII's Reformation, the Church was by far the biggest landowner in London.

The great landlords built churches as investments. The Earl of Bedford saw the merit of that idea for his Covent Garden development. He told his architect not to be too extravagant, though, and to build the token church like a barn. Inigo Jones is said to have replied, "it will be the finest barn in Europe."

From inspiration both godly and worldly, church-building contributed the city's greatest glories, most notably the triumphant legacy of Sir Christopher Wren. Eighty seven churches were lost in the Great Fire of 1666. In 30 years, Wren rebuilt 51 of them, the crowning achievement being the new St. Paul's Cathedral set among the modest dwellings of Ludgate Hill. Financed by a tax on coal, Wren had first call on the quarries of Portland in Dorset and used 1 million tons of their stone.

Legend has it that when Wren asked for a stone to mark a key position on the St Paul's building site, a labourer brought a fragment of gravestone inscribed *Resurgam* – "I shall arise" – happily apt for the project. Wren commissioned Caius Cibber to repeat it under a phoenix pediment (above).

Beneath the inner Baroque Dome of St Paul's (right), decorated by Sir James Thornhill with scenes of the saint's life. During the Blitz, an incendiary bomb started a small fire in a timber supporting the outer dome, the most noble shape on the City's skyline. An observant, precariously positioned fireman extinguished it – a diligent response to Winston Churchill's standing instruction, "save that church".

It was usual for great churches to be built over centuries by generations of devotees. St Paul's was built in 40 years by one architect, Sir Christopher Wren – and his salary was cut when Parliament decided that the work was going too slowly. The stone spiral staircase (far right) is under the clock of the south-west tower.

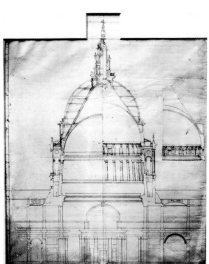

There was another burst of activity after 1711 when lawlessness in the suburbs was blamed on the lack of churches. Then Nicholas Hawksmoor, Wren's pupil, would make his mark as a church architect, and James Gibbs too. A further proliferation came when suburban churches were built from the proceeds of selling off now hugely-valuable sites in the City where there were no longer resident parishioners to pay the bills.

The Reformation had released church builders from any obligation to follow the traditional Gothic ground plan. Ecclesiastical architecture came to reflect fashionable styles, and the attitudes of the congregations to their faiths. Churches could be substantial statements exuding authority through tall towers and steeples, or more relaxed and private approaches to belief. The sturdy blocks of the non-conformists, Methodists and Baptists, spoke of a moral fervour which eschewed the grandeur of temples. Refugee groups such as Huguenots and Jews tended to worship discreetly, lest outward display attract the bigotry from which they had fled.

By the end of the 19th century, there were more than 4,000 places of worship in London, and a start had been made on "the finest church that has been built for centuries," the Roman Catholic Westminster Cathedral in Victoria, a neo-Byzantine design that took shape in just seven years. Funds were limited and interior decoration was left to future generations. That work continues to this day, while workers from the surrounding office blocks enjoy their breaks in the Italianate atmosphere of an adjoining piazza.

ROMAN CATHOLIC CATHEDRAL WESTMINSTER.

Just down Victoria Street from the Anglican and Gothic abbey of Westminster, the Roman Catholic church built a new cathedral in a purposely contrasting style. The architect undertook a "grand tour" of Italy, Greece, and Turkey to find inspiration; the materials he used are essentially English – London brick and Portland stone. JOHN FRANCIS BENTLEY, 1903

Southwark Cathedral, confined now by London Bridge, railway tracks, office buildings and Borough Market, lays claim to being the oldest Gothic church in London. The prosperity by which it acquired "fine monuments of great antiquity," as Samuel Pepys described them, came from its control of a landing wharf on the river. Among its more modern treasures is the 1903 "Creation Window" (right) by Henry Holiday in the pre-Raphaelite style. The six bands signify the six days of the biblical Creation.

Only in 1850 was the Catholic Hierarchy
restored in England, after 300 years of
suppression. As the faith burgeoned, the
Brompton Oratory, inside and out the
most Italianate of London churches,
became its fashionable centre.
HERBERT GRIBBLE, 1884

ST MARY ABCHURCH, BY WREN, HAS AN
ALTARPIECE BY GRINLING GIBBONS. 1686

ST DUNSTAN'S-IN-THE-EAST. WREN'S
TOWER DOMINATES. 1697

ST NICHOLAS COLE ABBEY (WREN)
AWAITING RECONSTRUCTION. 1677

CHRIST CHURCH, SPITALFIELDS.
A FINE HAWKSMOOR CHURCH. 1714

ST GEORGE-IN-THE-EAST. A HAWKSMOOR
TOWER SURROUNDED BY A SHELL. 1729

ST MARY WOOLNOTH. AN UNUSUALLY
"SECULAR" HAWKSMOOR CHURCH. 1727

ST MARTIN-IN-THE-FIELDS, BY JAMES
GIBBS AND ITALIAN DECORATORS. 1726

ST PAUL, COVENT GARDEN. INIGO
JONES'S ANCHOR TO THE PIAZZA. 1633

ST MARY-LE-BOW. WREN'S TOWER
HOUSED BOW BELLS. 1680

Jews were forbidden from building on a
main road; thus the courtyard gateway to
the oldest surviving English synagogue, off
Bevis Marks in the City. On the site of an
abbot's town house, the synagogue was
built by Joseph Avis, a Quaker carpenter,
on the authority of the Puritan Oliver
Cromwell, to serve a community of
Spanish and Portuguese Sephardic Jews.
The nearby Princelet Street Synagogue
(above), built behind a Huguenot
townhouse of 1722, was abandoned in
the 1960s.

Whitechapel (above) was usually the first
sanctuary for Jewish refugees. Followers
of Progressive Judaism in north-west
London built a new synagogue in
Wembley (right) in 2004.

# A new wave of worship

## POST-WAR CHURCHES

Perforated cladding at St Paul's on Southwark's Brandon Estate (top right); "baby" shades of pink and blue at St Paul's, Stratford (below right); and copious illumination for Congregationalists in Poplar (below).

In the eager rebuilding after World War II, places of worship were still a required community fixture, and ancient parishes and new housing estates adopted and adapted the design idioms of the day. "Light and bright" was the brief; blond woods and clean lines – tastes from Scandinavia that were influencing home-making – entered the church-builders' vocabularies.

The Baitul Futuh Mosque in the southern suburb of Morden (above) claims to be the largest mosque in western Europe. Its 52-ft. diameter dome is clad in stainless steel. Towards the end of World War II, King George VI donated the land that became the site of the Regent's Park Mosque (above, left) as a tribute to the Indian Muslims who fought and died defending the British Empire. The building, designed by the architect of Liverpool's Roman Catholic cathedral, was paid for by Saudi Arabia and the Gulf States.
SIR FREDERICK GIBBERD, 1978

Shri Swaminarayan Mandir in Neasden, North London (left), is Europe's first traditional Hindu temple. The intricacy of the design was matched by the complexities of the logistics: 5,000 tons of Bulgarian limestone and Italian marble shipped to India to be carved by 1,500 craftsmen in Gujurat and Rajasthan, and transported on as 26,000 pieces; no use to be made of sandstone, the traditionally favoured material, because of London pollution and rainfall; nor of steel as Vedic principles ban ferrous metals.

# Closed shops, free traders

Goldsmiths' Hall, damaged in
World War II, is refurbished
(above) ready for the 1951 Festival
of Britain.

## LIVERY COMPANIES

Governance of the City of London emanates not from a City Hall, but from the Guildhall, a name signifying the traditional power base in the Square Mile's millennium of growth. The guilds, now known as the City Livery Companies, were trade unions, operating closed shops that decided who should work and who should not, ensuring that sons might follow fathers into protected professions, controlling the apprenticeships that qualified craftsmen; fixing prices, wages and working conditions; controlling the quality of goods and manufactures. The upper echelons became liverymen, entitled to be freemen of the City of London, responsible still for electing the Lord Mayor and the Sheriffs.

Members of 100-odd companies built the City, armed it, fed it, and clothed it. They brought in its wealth and paid its bills. Since money talks, the men who rose to be Masters and Wardens were more likely to be merchants than artisans, and those leaders, travelled and sophisticated, housed their fraternities in style.

Their halls were built with competitive pride, then lavishly appointed with gifts from kings and ambassadors who sought favours at their banquets, and bequests from retirees gratefully acknowledging the source of their wealth. But many of these historic buildings were

The Drapers' Company, makers and merchants of woollen cloth, have been among the richest and most charitable of livery companies. Their present premises are a largely-Victorian rebuilding after fire damage. In the double-height Hall, portraits of royals hang among marble columns below a ceiling painted with Shakespearean scenes. HERBERT WILLIAMS, 1870.

An earlier Fishmongers' Hall was demolished to make way for the rebuilding of London Bridge; the present one stands alongside it. One of the most imposing livery halls, it has the proudest location of all, on the waterfront that enriched its founders. HENRY ROBERTS, 1834

# MONUMENTS TO MERCHANTS

The protective self-interests that prompted establishment of the City guilds have long since been rendered obsolete. More selfless activities keep them active: their inherited wealth supports schools, colleges, and charities concerned with the modern versions of their founders' trades.

GOLDSMITHS' HALL, FOSTER LANE.
PHILIP HARDWICK, 1835

1835. ARMOURERS' HALL, COLEMAN
STREET. J.H. GOOD, 1840

SADDLERS' HALL, GUTTER LANE.
L. SYLVESTER SULLIVAN, 1958

VINTNERS' HALL, UPPER THAMES STREET.
EDWARD AND ROGER JERMAN, 1671

in the path of the Great Fire, and many more took a beating in the Blitz. After both traumas, sensitive rebuilding and restoration preserved precious London legacies.

From a city-planning point of view, a downside of the power of the companies was jealous protection of their small parcels of land. After the Great Fire, Wren envisaged rebuilding the city astride open avenues. The guilds were loud among the vested interests that would not make way for his clear-cutting. Later, while the rest of London bulldozed its way through slums and obsolescence to make itself workable, such venerable City institutions continued to resist restructuring. The City remains a maddening maze, testing even London's legendarily-focussed cab-drivers to find ways through its pockets of heritage and high-rise.

The Goldsmiths' celebrated silverware being prepared for display (above).

Fraternal dining is at the heart of livery company culture. The Haberdashers do it in a contemporary version of a great hall where oak panelling sits among modern structural technology. This, the Haberdashers' fourth hall in a 500-year history, is in West Smithfield.
MICHAEL HOPKINS & PARTNERS, 2002

# Feeding the metropolis

## THE MARKETS

Much of old London's food came from nearby: from market gardens in Westminster and Brompton, from dairy farms around Notting Hill. Drovers could walk their herds and flocks into town from Essex, Kent, and the Midlands. London streets still bear the names of distribution centres: Poultry, Honey Lane where beekeepers lived, and Haymarket where fodder for the city's horses was sold on. But three main wholesale markets came

Bustling Billingsgate, beside the Monument commemorating the 1666 Fire of London, put the fish on Londoners' tables. The porters' load-bearing leather hats were said to derive from those that protected Agincourt archers.

to dominate the fresh food trades – Billingsgate for fish, Covent Garden for fruit and vegetables, Smithfield for meat.

Billingsgate operated for 1,000 years from a wharf beside London Bridge, for most of the time as a ramshackle shanty town of sheds and stalls. A proper market built in 1850 was quickly inadequate to serve London's appetite and, 25 years later, Sir Horace Jones, the City's official architect, put up a sturdy iron structure under mansard roofs embellished with golden dolphin weathervanes. Mutterings about the site's deficiencies continued for another 100 years, finally resulting in a move to a purpose-built complex on the Isle of Dogs. Richard Rogers did the make-over of Sir Horace's building, now heritage listed, to serve financial dealing more akin to the City's main interests.

Street traders first laid out their wares in Covent Garden in the 1650s. The market just grew and grew to spread over 30 acres. When darkness fell and the produce stalls closed, less savoury trades came to light – gambling and whoring: John Cleland's cheerfully promiscuous heroine, Fanny Hill, had her base here. Order was imposed in the 19th century and the graceful iron arches, expansive glazing and Tuscan arcades that are now landmarks on the London tourist trail filled the piazza, while visitors to the opera house next door picked up their buttonholes and bouquets at the Floral Hall next door. The market moved to disused railway yards at Nine Elms, Vauxhall, in 1974.

Billingsgate was noted for the foul language of its porters, Covent Garden had a licentious reputation. There was an altogether darker side to Smithfield. A horse and cattle market since the 13th century, it was also a public execution ground for 400 years and a place where "witches and heretics" were roasted or boiled alive. The slaughter of animals continued at Smithfield until 1855. Then Sir Horace Jones built the honest, functional Victorian buildings that still serve as London's central meat market.

Scant regard for Covent Garden's architectural treasures during the daily distribution of London's fruit and vegetables (left). Picturesque practice gave way to functional orderliness when the market moved to Vauxhall (below left). NEW COVENT GARDEN MARKET: GOLLINS, MELVIN, WARD & PARTNERS, 1974.

Spitalfields Market served the City's residents for centuries. The tidy scene (above) marks the opening of its new covered market in the 1920s. Being nearer to the docks than Covent Garden, Spitalfields specialized in imported fruit; its cellars were heated to ripen bananas. Smithfield Meat Market (right) is the only major City market still going about its business.

# One-stop shopping

## DEPARTMENT STORES

The "Tudor" timbers of Liberty's in Regent Street (left) are not just stick-on conceits. They were salvaged from warships and are crucial to the structure built in the 1920s. Passers-by at the arch over Kingly Street watch as the hour strikes, and St George jabs the dragon with his lance.
E.T. & E.S. HALL, 1926

The original Harrods store (below) grew out over the gardens of Knightsbridge townhouses where the family lived, and remained in business while the new store was built (above). Harrods now occupies a whole city block, of 4.5 acres.
STEVENS & MUNT, 1905

It was hardly relaxing retail therapy. There would be a boot in the dimly-lit window to show that here was a shoe-maker, a straw hat to signify a milliner's. The lady out to buy a new outfit might need to travel all over town, to a street specialising in lace and silks, to others noted for parasols, petticoats, gloves. She would have to haggle over prices, and wait for her choices to be made to order.

Shopping became easier as diversities of traders concentrated, in bazaars in the poorer areas, and fashionable arcades in the West End – Burlington Arcade and Nash's colonnaded Regent Street. Then, in the mid-19th century, the sweatshops of the East End, mostly worked by Jewish immigrants, began pouring out ready-made clothes. Modern retailing began, and the scene was set for department stores.

William Whiteley was first to set up shop, in Westbourne Grove where a suburb was burgeoning around the Paddington terminus of the first underground railway. A draper by trade, Whiteley bought up adjoining shops until his claim to be the "universal provider" was justified by a stock of commodities and services ranging from perambulators to undertaking. By 1900, his turnover was over £1 million a year.

Across the park, the grocer Charles Harrod applied the same strategy, buying out his neighbours in the Brompton Road, Knightsbridge. The drapers of Oxford and Regent Streets followed suit: Marshall and Snelgrove, Dickins and Jones, Swan and Edgar, Debenham and Freebody (reached on the beguiling telephone number, Mayfair One). Smarter suburbanites could do all their shopping under one roof at Arding and Hobbs in Clapham,

A feast of mosaics and Art Nouveau tiles in Harrods Food Halls (top). Selfridges, too, dressed in style (above); this illuminated floral aisle was the setting for its birthday celebration in 1934.
SELFRIDGES: R.F. BURNHAM, DANIEL BURNHAM, SIR JOHN BURNET, FROM 1907

Peter Jones in Sloane Square (facing page) was deemed one of the best buildings of the 1930s. Here, in the 1960s, an escalator was installed to ease traffic on the glazed spiral staircase.
W. CRABTREE, 1938

and at Barkers in Kensington, which sold enough linen "to put a bandage round the earth."

As iron and steel construction and curtain-walling allowed larger and larger display windows, as electricity supplied theatrical lighting and power for lifts and escalators, department stores became purpose-built rather than clusters of small shops. Whiteley's and Harrods were rebuilt as Edwardian retail temples. And American hard-sell came on the scene with the arrival of Gordon Selfridge, an experienced Chicago retailer, in Oxford Street, in 1909.

Selfridges was and is an entire city block, New York-style. Enormous Ionic columns stand proud of a steel frame, over a ground floor where Selfridge's Chicago-trained window dresser arranged still-lifes of merchandise. He made space for a soda fountain and a bargain basement, and inducted his staff into the "have-a-nice-day" attitude. Shopping became pleasurable, not least through another innovation for the ladies — attractive powder rooms, with toilets. Whereas a man in need could hurry to his club, a pub or a dark alley, before department stores women who were out and about had had few such opportunities for relief.

Joined-up retailing, bringing a variety of merchandise to the attention of fashionable shoppers under one roof, was, and is, stylishly practised in Piccadilly's Burlington Arcade, a long corridor of bow fronts, tenanted by independent traders, built along the boundary of Lord Cavendish's London address, Burlington House. Curiously, modern department stores have revived this manner of marketing, with single-brand franchises dominating the sales floors.

SAMUEL WARE, 1819

The suburbs shared in Edwardian prosperity, encouraging Arding and Hobbs to plant a statement store on modest Lavender Hill in Clapham. It is seen here in 1934 (right, above) when, in Piccadilly, Simpson's men's store (right) was being "engineered" in welded steel.

ARDING AND HOBBS: J. GIBSON, 1910
SIMPSON'S: JOSEPH EMBERTON, 1935

Cast-iron colonnades once stepped out to the street along Nash's original Quadrant – but they were not good for business. On the right of the photograph, an archway surmounted by Tuscan columns allows entry to Swallow Street without interrupting the flow of the terrace.

# Nash's triumphal way

## REGENT STREET

It was a masterstroke of urban planning, spanning the town from Pall Mall to its northern exits. It was the most effective, exquisite street in London, one that might have ranked with Europe's finest boulevards. But Regent Street, the grandest expression of Georgian style, was not to have the protection it deserved.

 Its nascence was in the extravagant ambitions of the Prince Regent. His grand home, Carlton House, was somewhat blocked to the north. In 1811, the lease of Marylebone Park, a mile or so away, where Elizabeth I had hunted with the Duke of Anjou and Lords Albemarle and Townshend fought messy duels, reverted to the Crown. Why not a country villa there, and a "royal mile" to connect the two? Furthermore, the road would distance the grand houses of St James's from teeming, low-life Soho.

 The Regent's favourite architect, John Nash, sketched out New Street, as it was named on the early plans. First, Nash cleared a mean precinct in front of Carlton House to create the formality of Waterloo Place, and lined what would be Lower Regent Street with classical buildings. At Piccadilly, there could not be a mere crossing, there had to be a splendid confluence. Nash built a "circus," with curved

buildings disguising the angles, emphasizing his new street's right of way.

Then the road had to jink left and right – there wasn't the budget to demolish everything in a straight line north. And it was here that Nash gave the street its distinguishing characteristic: a Quadrant, a leisurely curving quarter circle where Doric columns at the pavements' edges supported colonnades protecting window shoppers. Nash was so anxious that the speculators and tenants he needed should not alter his plans that he financed the project himself. He had in mind the arcades of Milan and Bologna and, indeed, the original Covent Garden piazza; and he wrote ingenuously of the socializing opportunities, whereby loungers on the balconies would chat with the passengers of carriages stalled in the fashionable traffic.

From the Quadrant, a straight thoroughfare northward, crossing Oxford Street at another soft-edged "circus". And where a further left/right chicane was required, he placed the circular, columned form of All Souls, Langham Place, in the line of sight, camouflaging the corner. Then the broad avenue of Portland Place, mostly the work of the Adam brothers, led to the semi-circle of Park Crescent and entry to the park, newly named Regent's Park, where Nash's terraces of wealthy homes were considered "the most beautiful estate in London.".

Regent Street was not a project that Nash could complete alone. Property developers had to pay the bills, and had their own choices of architects. But as the Regent's appointee, Nash could influence and over-ride, insisting on a church here and there or a vista, like the one through to the colonnaded Theatre Royal on the Haymarket, to relieve the commercial frontages.

By 1823, Regent Street was completed. It was not long, though, before the profit imperative overwhelmed the vision. Within a quarter of a century, the arcades were dismantled: not enough light for our window displays, the shopkeepers said, and street-walkers lurk among them, offending the passing trade. Extra floors erupted through a carefully-considered skyline, Portland stone buildings punctuated graceful, uniform facades of stucco; and the expanses of glass allowed by curtain wall construction pushed Regent Street toward being a nondescript 20th-century trading post. The broad brushstroke of Nash's vision remains. The humane Regency harmony has gone.

In Nash's time, retailing was a matter of small businesses serving local residents. Regent Street's very fashionability, attracting shoppers from around the world, quickly overwhelmed that modus. Shops coalesced into stores – one of them requiring a Soho hostel for its 200 sales assistants.

# Rooms to rent

## HOTELS

An overload of Art Deco at the
Strand Palace Hotel. Much of this
internally-lit glass foyer is now
preserved in the Victoria and
Albert Museum.
OLIVER BERNARD, 1929

The Midland Grand (below), the most
impressive Victorian railway hotel,
had magnificent public rooms, but no
en-suite bathrooms and only coal fires
to heat the bedrooms. Nevertheless, it
hosted passengers disembarking at
St Pancras until the 1930s. The
Piccadilly Hotel (right) was decorated
to the taste of Edwardian big
spenders. Achieving the required
splendour bankrupted its owners.
MIDLAND GRAND HOTEL: SIR
GEORGE GILBERT SCOTT, 1873.
PICCADILLY HOTEL: NORMAN
SHAW, 1908.

Visiting gentlemen might stay at their clubs, off-loading their families at the well-staffed townhouses of their friends; lesser travellers put up at inns or lodging houses. But when the Great Exhibition of 1851 triggered London's first tourist boom, and the new railways brought the capital within convenient range of the rest of the nation, commercialized hospitality came of age.

The railway companies made the first moves. There had been modest accommodations at Euston, for visitors from Birmingham. Now, at Paddington and King's Cross, Victoria and Charing Cross, ever-larger hotels appeared, culminating in the massive Midland Grand that George Gilbert Scott built as a frontage for St Pancras Station.

Hydraulic lifts made high floors accessible, so Scott could use the lofty vertical lines that flattered the Gothic style. His competitors often went for a "French" look, acknowledging that Paris was ahead in building sophisticated hotels. New York, too, provided trends: along with lifts and electric lighting, the Savoy Hotel had 80 bathrooms (at the Westminster Palace Hotel in Victoria Street, there were just 14 bathrooms for 300 bedrooms).

At different times different parts of the city attracted hotels in clusters. In Bloomsbury, the architect Charles Fitzroy Doll added a Victorian face to the Regency restraint of Russell Square with the red brick and terracotta Russell Hotel (1898); then an Edwardian one with the Imperial, a decade later.

Huge hotels were built in Northumberland Avenue, making Trafalgar Square, briefly, the city's welcome centre (two of them later became office blocks). Nearby, the

Cecil (1886) stretched from the Embankment to the Strand to take the title of Europe's largest hotel. It was rebuilt as Shell-Mex House in 1931.

Then the carriage trade moved west, as elegance in London tended to do. A small hotel in Mayfair grew up to become Claridge's, with the most glamorous of all guest lists. The architects of Cesar Ritz's Paris hotel echoed that city's street style with an arcaded frontage to the London Ritz on Piccadilly. The Ritz's facings of Norwegian granite dress London's first steel-framed building (1906). And on Park Lane grand private mansions made way for grand hotels where the aristocratic lineage survives in the names: Grosvenor House and the Dorchester.

As London shook off its down-trodden, war-torn image and sprang into the "swinging sixties," Park Lane found room for a high-rise newcomer, the 405-ft London Hilton (1963), whose rooftop bar allowed glimpses into the gardens of Buckingham Palace. Other international chains built formulaic hotels at the airports and along the highways into town.

But that formula was becoming boring to the jet set. The smarter places to stay were smaller, more intimate. The fashion designer Anouska Hempel converted a Bayswater row of Georgian townhouses into a Japanese-minimal, Zen-flavoured "boutique" hotel. (She had already made a success of Blakes in Chelsea, where guests enjoyed the other extreme of oriental style, a "sensory overload" of decadent Raj opulence.) Then came the Sanderson and the St Martin's Lane, converted from a wallpaper showroom and an office building by Ian Schrager, known for the trendy New York night club, Studio 54. The appeal here is surreal detailing by the designer Philippe Starck. "Wit" and "irony" – unlikely words in the hotel-keepers' lexicon – are part of the sales pitch.

In the early 1800s, a small hotel in Brook Street, Mayfair, did well enough to encourage the owner to acquire and incorporate adjacent houses. William Claridge, a butler by training, added the business to his own modest hotel in the same block. The Savoy hotel group bought the untidy complex, demolished it, and built Claridge's on the site.
C.W. STEPHENS, 1898

THE LANGHAM DOMINATES ONE OF LONDON'S BROADEST
AVENUES, PORTLAND PLACE. J. GILES AND JAMES MURRAY, 1865

THE SAVOY. THE STAINLESS STEEL FASCIA WAS A 1920s
ART DECO UP-DATING. THOMAS COLCUTT, 1889

CLARIDGE'S IN 1925. ITS ELEGANT STAIRCASE LED TO A
MUCH-USED ROYAL SUITE. C.W. STEPHENS, 1898

THE RITZ. FROM UNDER THE AWNINGS, VIEWS ACROSS
GREEN PARK. CHARLES MEWES, ARTHUR J. DAVIES, 1906

THE GRAND, A TRAFALGAR SQUARE HOTEL THAT BECAME
AN OFFICE BLOCK. FRANCIS AND J.E. SAUNDERS, 1881

THE STRAND PALACE OF 1909, REPLACED 20 YEARS LATER
BY A 700-ROOM HOTEL BUILT BY THE J.LYONS COMPANY.

Ian Schrager and Philippe Starck honed their talent for dramatic make-overs at a run-down New York hotel, The Royalton, a roach-ridden refuge near Times Square that they turned into one of the city's most fashionable venues. In London, they transformed premises untroubled by their pasts. The Sanderson, in Berners Street, is named for the furnishings company it replaced. Behind the modernist façade – in its own right, this was one of the few admired London buildings of the 1960s – Starck created a lobby whose delight is in the details (above). The backdrop is an 18th-century opera curtain.

Eyes in the backs of their bar stools at
the Sanderson Long Bar – 82 ft. long, in
fact (left). Here, the mood is cool and
calm. At the St Martin's Lane Hotel, the
other Schrager/Starck creation, changing
coloured lighting sets the tone in the
Light Bar (above), under photographs of
highly-expressioned faces. The
Sanderson's en-suite bathrooms are glass
boxes, though the modest bather can
draw a sheer curtain (far left).

# Out to dinner

## RESTAURANTS

Charles Dickens was among the gentlemen who regularly dined on John Simpson's roast beef and saddles of mutton. The restaurant moved to its current premises after the road-widening of the Strand in 1900.

For many less-eminent Londoners between the wars, a Lyons Corner House (right, at Coventry Street) was their first experience of eating out, an adventure made comfortable by crisply-outfitted "nippies" (below).

Eating out was a dreary process for most Londoners in the early 19th century. Gentlemen could dine handsomely at their clubs, but for the rest there was the choice of a place at a long, littered communal table in a smoke-filled tavern or chop-house, or eating on the street where hundreds of peddlers offered oysters, hot eels, mutton pies, and pigs' trotters. Women stayed at home.

The railways brought civilising touches. Station hotels introduced dining rooms that welcomed women travellers, and at his hotel in Piccadilly, Cesar Ritz offered the intimacy of separate tables – and a celebrity chef, Auguste Escoffier. The Criterion and Gaiety theatres opened restaurants so that dinner and a show became the rounded evening out. The Italian Gatti brothers, themselves theatre owners, added live music to the dining experience at their Charing Cross restaurant.

Meat and gravy – that was the *plat du jour;* Londoners were noted carnivores. Simpson's in the Strand served it with a flourish from a gleaming, rolling carving trolley. But in Soho, the menu was changing. Here, French, German, Italian, Greek, Turkish immigrants were beguiling their compatriots with homeland cooking. Native Londoners who dared to venture into the dark alleys east of Regent Street discovered new worlds of tastes.

As plant-draped "palm courts" and plush velvet banquettes became the dining habitats of extravagant Edwardians, cheerful teashops served the new generation of respectable working women – typists and telephonists. In 1909, the J. Lyons chain super-sized the concept. When its first Corner House, in Coventry Street, had finished absorbing

surrounding premises, it could seat 4,500 customers of modest means among chandeliers and gilded balustrades, trappings traditionally reserved for more prosperous customers.

Sir Terence Conran revived the idea of giant restaurants in the 1990s, opening Quaglino's in the vast and obsolete ballroom of a St James's hotel. And the growth of Conran's stylish food empire had the serendipitous effect of preserving other landmark buildings: a redbrick stable block in Marylebone, a historically important garage/workshop in Chelsea, and the glamorously eccentric Michelin Building, where London's first motorists changed their fragile tyres before heading west for country weekends.

# A welcome and a warm beer

## PUBS

The gossip of journalists and lawyers was the appeal of Ye Olde Cheshire Cheese off Fleet Street (below), where big-spending was encouraged by a house parrot mimicking the sound of a popping champagne cork. Show business fuels the conversation at the Salisbury (right), close to a dozen West End stage doors. Its Victorian splendour is well preserved: cut and frosted glass, burnished brass and red plush, all gleaming under Art Nouveau lamps.

As corner sites were their usual location, pubs were the city's landmarks, its navigational beacons. A Victorian Londoner who was asked for directions was more likely to indicate the route by way of pub names than street signs. And the names are an etymological distraction in their own right, dubiously associating kings and cardinals, judges and generals with the hospitality on offer.

Inns, taverns, and alehouses are stages in the evolution of public houses – and the notorious gin shops whose rough liquor rotted the livers and lives of the London poor until taxation controlled them in the 1750s. Even impolite society needs lubrication, and as the water was undrinkable and tea and coffee were heavily taxed, pubs serving beer – made with hops from nearby Kent – became social centres. If there were community or labour issues to discuss, the pub was a cheerier place to do it than the church hall. Pubs served as informal job centres: builders looked for work at The Bricklayer's Arms; joiners at The Carpenter's Rest, whose landlords were often veterans of those trades. The downside of that, as far as temperance campaigners were concerned, was that paydays happened in the pub too, and often not much of the earnings reached home and family.

By mid-Victorian times, when there was a pub for every 400 Londoners, the interior design had settled into a formula. A horseshoe shaped bar around a mirror-reflected display of bottles – more or less exotic, depending on the clientele – with the drinking area screen-divided into a public bar, a saloon bar and a more intimate "snug." The drinks were the same, but the prices went up according to the level of comfort – from sawdust on the floor to carpet, from hard benches to armchairs.

As Londoners got out and about more, as restaurants, music halls, and theatres competed for the new spending on leisure, pubs raised their game, with welcoming polished stone facades, discreet etched-glass windows, gleaming brass chandeliers and mahogany columns.

Even in the classier 19th century residential developments, such as Thomas Cubitt's Pimlico, pubs were planned in as standard fittings, considered as necessary for the community as fire and police stations.

The Prospect of Whitby hangs out over the river at Wapping. Earlier patrons, in the 16th century, were river thieves and smugglers whose custom earned it the name, the Devil's Tavern.

Prime position in Chelsea – a corner site for Sunday morning drinkers in 1949.

# Members only

## GENTLEMEN'S CLUBS

The Carlton Club, the centre for Conservative Party internal politicking, was at the heart of the Pall Mall corridor of power. It was bombed in World War II when the members moved to premises in St James's Street. SIDNEY SMIRKE, GEORGE BASEVI, 1855.

Rules for members of White's (right) were written in the 1730s, making it the oldest of the St James's clubs; and it was the grandest, with a succession of kings and prime ministers on the rolls. In the most recent of the great clubhouses, the Royal Automobile Club (below), the traditional mahogany and leather made way for gilt and brocade – as if lady motorists were expected.

The elegant few acres known as St James's, from Lower Regent Street across to Green Park, were, and to a great degree still are, a male preserve – Gentlemen's London. Here were the aristocratic townhouses and bachelors' chambers of men-about-town. Bespoke shirtmakers, bootmakers, and hatters set up shop to serve them, alongside cigar and wine merchants. And underlining this discrete community, the imposing gentlemen's clubs along St James's Street and Pall Mall, a confident display of classical styles on a grand scale.

Previously, select taverns and coffee houses had been the meeting places where political agendas were set, business negotiated and inheritances lost at the card table. But with 1820s tax cuts, coffee became affordable by the lower classes. The spittoons overflowing, the air thick with cheap tobacco smoke, gentlemen moved on. Their new refuges were established in Pall Mall as not-for-profit collectives, where they could fraternise grandly yet affordably.

Memberships derived from common interests. Rule 6 of the Travellers' Club charter stated, "No person shall be considered eligible … who shall not have travelled out of the British Isles to a distance of at least 500 miles from London in a direct line." Sir Charles Barry modelled their clubhouse (1832) on the Villa Pandolfini in Florence. Barry then built the Reform Club (1841), copying the Farnese Palace, for Liberal members of the Lords and Commons. Clean water, still then a luxury, came from the club's own artesian well. The kitchen was under the command of Alexis Soyer, an early celebrity chef. Next door was the Carlton, for high Tories.

John Nash built the United Service Club (1826) for officers "not under the rank of major, or commander in the navy." Artists and literary men gathered at the

An Athenaeum interior.
Artists, writers, and scientists
were the core membership.
Book-lined libraries are
favourite rooms; Athene,
Goddess of Wisdom, is poised
over the front door.

Athenaeum, a Grecian style block by Decimus Burton (1830). Twentieth-century interests intruded in 1911, when the Royal Automobile Club opened the last and largest clubhouse on Pall Mall, with Turkish baths and a marble swimming pool in the basement

Nearby in St James's Street were the older, more raffish clubs where quality of birth rather than shared interests was the qualification for membership: White's named after the coffee house it replaced in 1736, and Boodle's, for serious gambling – "the bane of half the nobility."

THERE IS A STEEL FRAME BEHIND THE ROYAL AUTOMOBILE
CLUB'S CLASSICAL FRONTAGE. MEWES & DAVIES, 1911

BROOKS'S CLUB IN ST JAMES'S STREET – ANOTHER CLUB
ONCE NOTED FOR ITS GAMING. HENRY HOLLAND, 1778.

THE ATHENAEUM – AS THE ROMAN NAME SUGGESTS, FOR
THE INTELLECTUAL ELITE. DECIMUS BURTON, 1830

THE DEVONSHIRE CLUB'S FORMER HOME IN ST JAMES'S
STREET. BENJAMIN AND PHILIP WYATT, 1827

BOODLE'S – THE ELEGANT AND ONLY LONDON BUILDING BY
THIS ARCHITECT. JOHN CRUNDEN, 1776

THE REFORM CLUB – FOR POLITICAL RADICALS, A PALAZZO
AROUND A GLAZED COURTYARD. SIR CHARLES BARRY, 1841

# A place in town

The flames of 1666 flickered and died at Blackfriars. The firebreak was probably one of the gardens – indeed parks – of the great houses lining the north bank of the Thames – Essex House, Arundel House, Savoy Palace, Somerset House. Safe, too, were the London homes of the Earl of Bedford and Lord Burleigh, also overlooking the river from the Strand.

A Renaissance palace built for a Duke of Somerset was subsumed into London's first large office block. The Thames once lapped its terraces. Here, construction of the Victoria Embankment is changing the outlook.

Such places had often been the London palaces of bishops, a rich and high-living stratum of society. Confiscated at the Reformation, they were handed out to the great patrician families. Though their fortunes were fed by vast country estates, these nobles required a presence in town, close to the money-machine of the City and the ear of the monarch. What's more, they had sons and daughters to introduce into Society, maybe to marry and so merge great landholdings, as the Southamptons and Russells did to create a property portfolio that included Covent Garden and Bloomsbury.

Remains of the pre-Elizabethan London mansions are few (the Earl of Arundel, for instance, preferred the income to be derived from four new streets on his estate to retaining Arundel House). Architects and their patrons toured Europe, noting the grandeur of the aristocrats' *hotels* in Paris, and the splendour of Palladianism in the Veneto. The first "celebrity" architects, Inigo Jones and Christopher Wren, brought continental influences to muddled old London.

Jones built the chapel that began the still on-going transformation of the Duke of Somerset's House, first built in 1547. It gained a frontage on the Strand with an imposing French-style gateway, a courtyard, Corinthian pavilions, a gallery along the waterfront. Then major demolition made way for a government building that grew so large it threatened Whitehall's dominance as the bureaucracy's power base.

For a while Somerset House accommodated the Royal Academy, which eventually settled in another patrician palace, in Piccadilly. That is Burlington House, built as a somewhat rustic block in the 1660s, then remodelled along strict Italianate lines 50 years later by the third Earl of Burlington. Burlington became an architect in his own right. The

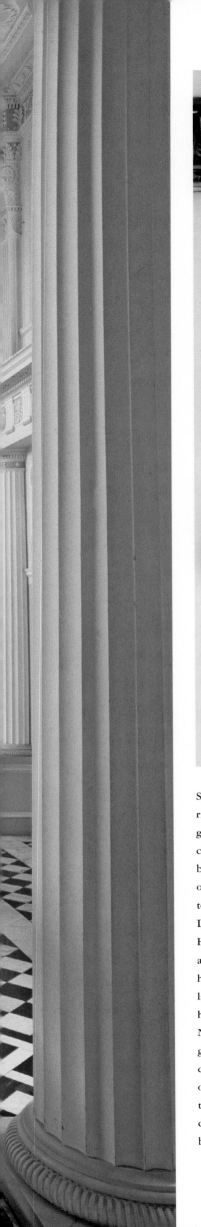

Syon House, in its own park beside the river approaching Richmond, had a gruesome early history. Henry VIII confined his wife Catherine Howard here before her execution; his own coffin burst open during an overnight stay on its way to Windsor. A one-time resident, the Duke of Somerset was taken from Syon House to be executed; Lady Jane Grey accepted the crown here, but was soon hanged. The peaceful house of today is largely the work of Robert Adam, hired in the 1760s by the Duke of Northumberland to impose classical grandeur on what had originally been a convent. This he demonstrated with rich ornamentation and the lofty coolness of the entrance hall, a marble-floored double cube where the Dying Gaul subsides between characteristic Adam columns.

country house he designed for himself in Chiswick pays handsome acknowledgement to his mentor, Palladio.

Preservation as galleries and museums saved other London mansions. Montagu House in Bloomsbury had a second, though brief, life as the British Museum; Hertford House in Manchester Square is now the home of the Wallace Collection; Apsley House, the Duke of Wellington's residence at Hyde Park Corner, proudly displays mementoes of his celebrated career; and Kenwood House, set in magnificent gardens beside Hampstead Heath, is a suburban treat. Crewe House in Curzon Street, greatly altered from its 18th-century beginnings but still one of Mayfair's most imposing buildings, is now the Saudi Embassy.

Mansions ringed the capital, but for home-hunting Lord Palmerston, Hertford House, just north of Oxford Street, was too "sadly out of the way" in 1808.

KENWOOD HOUSE, HAMPSTEAD. 1764

WITANHURST HOUSE, HIGHGATE. 1913

HERTFORD HOUSE, MANCHESTER SQUARE, 1788

The Duke of Wellington's personal treasures – war booty and tributes from allies and a grateful nation – remain at Apsley House, his home at Hyde Park Corner (left and above), now the Wellington Museum. Among a large collection of paintings are some outstanding Spanish works captured from Joseph Bonaparte at the Battle of Vitoria. The Iron Duke brought out his magnificent tableware every year for a banquet on the anniversary of the Battle of Waterloo. Robert Adam built the house in 1778; the duke's family, the Wellesleys, bought it, and James and Benjamin remodelled, enlarged, and refaced it, in Bath stone. Park Crescent (below) represented another kind of gracious London living, where pairs of Ionic columns outline the terraces John Nash built as the curvaceous entry to Regent's Park.

MARLBOROUGH HOUSE, PALL MALL, 1711

HOLLAND HOUSE, KENSINGTON. c.1606

# Ostentatious oases

## GARDEN SQUARES

A unique and relieving feature among the heavy, random, sometimes gloomy, concentration of London building is its garden squares, where terraces of tall, companionable residences overlook communal gardens. The notion came from Paris, where the grand houses – known, confusingly, to an English speaker as *hotels* – were built around courtyards – private patches of countryside in the city maze.

An Earl of Bedford had admired the Parisian examples; Inigo Jones, the king's Surveyor-General was commissioned to create one for him in London in the 1630s. But Jones's influences and inspiration came from Livorno in Italy. Thus Covent Garden has always been known as a *piazza,* recalling the long-gone colonnades with which the architect fronted the houses on two sides. To the south were the gardens of Bedford House; to the east, the Church of St Paul, behind Tuscan columns.

Although not truly a garden square – it was paved – Covent Garden was for a while among the most fashionable residential enclaves in London, encouraging other aristocrats to follow this lead into the property market. Their noble names – Southampton, Berkeley, Grosvenor – branded prestigious addresses where speculative builders would sometimes place

Montpelier Square, built on Knightsbridge fields in the 1840s, was not originally as grand as its warning notice later suggested. John Galsworthy's *The Forsyte Saga* gave it status. Soames Forsyte lived here.

A complex transaction between Earl Grosvenor and Thomas Cubitt, Pimlico's developer, comforted by Swiss bankers, inspired the building of Belgrave Square as an address to rival the most fashionable in Mayfair. The name came from a village on the earl's Leicestershire estate; its bricks were made from the clay on site. The first architect employed, in 1826, was Sir John Soane's pupil, George Basevi.

Office blocks, banks, and car showrooms now frame Berkeley Square. At one time it was the garden of a mansion on Piccadilly, and later the outlook for some of the finest Georgian houses in London, homes for Clive of India, William Pitt the Elder and Sydney Smirke, the architect. A few of the handsome old buildings survive. Alexander Munro's marble nymph, shown refreshing workers in the 1930s, was later more proudly positioned among the 200-year-old plane trees.

Kensington Square (below) was a daring development of the 1680s, an urban outpost among fields and farmlands. It acquired status and notable tenants when nearby Nottingham House became the royal residence of Kensington Palace.

The northern terrace of Cleveland Square
presents its elegant back to the garden.
The stuccoed, pillared frontage is even
grander, but now overlooks a 1950s
housing estate. Nevertheless, this is one
of the more desirable addresses in
Bayswater, as it was in Victorian times.

The newly-landscaped Leicester Square prepares for a grand reopening in 1874, around a marble fountain surmounted by a statue of Shakespeare. Developed in the 17th century as "a very handsome large square … graced with good built houses … resorted unto by gentry," Leicester Square had become squalid and dangerous – conditions which now threaten it again.

one particularly splendid residence for the plot's owner among the harmonious terraces. Inadvertently, perhaps, here was the business model by which the great aristocratic families would make continuing fortunes in London property. The key was leaseholds, at first set for 42 years. Then, title to the land and the buildings, which had rocketed in value in a city hard-pressed for space, reverted to the freeholder who could restart the profit cycle.

Socially, the garden squares were the equivalent of today's "gated" communities, self-contained enclaves, not troubled by the noisome presence of the underclasses, and with tradesmen esconced nearby to serve them. (At Covent Garden, though, the market got out of hand, driving away the fashionable residents, settling into a new role as London's premier distribution centre for fruit and vegetables – a not inappropriate reversion: the land had formerly been a convent garden.)

Garden squares were a significant step towards the humane patterns of Georgian London. They appeared all over town, to house the rising waves of prosperous professionals – merchants, lawyers, bankers. They are admired still, their frontages heritage-protected against anachronistic improvement – although the close observer will note that instead of one doorbell at each porticoed entrance, there will now be a plate of a dozen or more buzzers to serve the flat-owners who share what would have been a single-family space. And behind these grand terraces, their coach houses and stables have become mews houses, some of the city's most coveted residences.

# Breathing the air

## PARKS AND GARDENS

A welcome new playground where the filthy, tidal river had until recently licked at the background buildings (right): Victoria Embankment Gardens on the land reclaimed to cover Bazalgette's life-saving sewers. For London's nursemaids, the Broad Walks of Hyde Park and Kensington Gardens (below) were preferred routes for perambulation – safe zones except for flirtatious attention from the cavalrymen of Knightsbridge Barracks.

Building London has been a frenzied activity for a millennium, yet unbuilt London is the city's most remarkable feature, the envy of every other metropolis. It is possible to observe ducks nesting on the lake beside Downing Street and then walk briskly for an hour along tree-lined pathways, across lawns and alongside the Serpentine, maybe glimpsing an urban fox among the bushes, to the swan-graced Round Pond in Kensington Gardens. The city's growling business is on all sides but intrudes only in front of Buckingham Palace and at Hyde Park Corner's pedestrian underpass.

Deer still roam the 2,400 acres of Richmond Park, once a hunting field for Hampton Court Palace. The Heath at Hampstead, the Common at Clapham, the Park at Crystal Palace are out of bounds to the property developers, highlights among the 70 square miles of protected open spaces in Greater London. Some of it was church land impounded at the Dissolution of the Monasteries, some common land reserved for the people since medieval times, and some, bequests or purchases of manorial rights from the great landowners. Sir Sidney Waterlow, a Lord Mayor of London, gave his Highgate estate to the city in 1889; it should be "a garden for the gardenless," he insisted, with a scented garden for blind visitors to enjoy.

But it is the central royal legacies that particularly distinguish green London. The walk from Whitehall to Kensington is through four of them, St James's Park, Green Park, Hyde Park, and Kensington Gardens, all owed to the acquisitiveness of Henry VIII. He saw the potential of the boggy field at St James's as a starting point

for hunting that could end as far away as the hills of Hampstead, then added Green Park to this royal enclosure, and appropriated Hyde Park.

St James's Park got the most attention from later monarchs. Mulberry bushes were planted, in an attempt to furnish the court with home-made silk. Formal gardens were laid out, inspired by the landscaping of Versailles, an aviary built (thus, Birdcage Walk), and a Chinese pagoda that burned down during a fireworks display.

Regent's Park is another prize that Henry VIII picked up at the Dissolution. In the early 19th century, the Prince Regent encouraged its development as London's grandest housing estate. His favoured architect, John Nash, planned terraces that would look like palaces, among villas set in their own miniature parks. The plan was only partly fulfilled, but there is enough of Nash's work to suggest what might have been; and enough left of the nearly 500 acres for Londoners to enjoy their zoo, Queen Mary's Rose Garden, an open air theatre and a boating lake.

An estate at Kew was a favourite royal residence in the early 18th century. Successive occupants dabbled in exotic plantings, so the Royal Botanic Gardens is properly named. It became the nation's property in 1840 and grew from nine acres to 300. "Capability" Brown did early landscaping, Decimus Burton built the Palm House, and Sir William Chambers the Pagoda. A much-loved oasis for Londoners, Kew remains an important horticultural research centre. Much less well-groomed but equally appreciated, Hampstead Heath (right) came into the public domain after local residents won a long legal battle against the Lord of the Manor, in 1871.

Fashionable parades of riders, carriages, and couture once enlivened Hyde Park's Rotten Row (from *route de roi* – the king's road). By the 1930s, the traffic was much less formal.

# Places of honour

## MEMORIALS AND STATUES

In its dense, rich population of statuary, London pays tribute to a remarkably eclectic circle of influential figures and friends: American presidents, Polish fighter pilots who defended the city, Peter Pan and Charlie Chaplin who beguiled from stage and film, and every monarch since Elizabeth I (with the exception of the dishonoured King Edward VIII).

Naval and military heroes do best: Admiral Nelson dominating Trafalgar Square from his tall column; the Duke of Wellington in several appearances, one sardonically cast from captured French guns. Another tribute to him was London's first nude statue: the figure of Achilles, overlooking Apsley House, the Duke's home on the southern fringe of Hyde Park. A patriotic group calling themselves "the Women of England" put aside their modesty to pay for it. A fig leaf was added later.

Every suburb has its war memorial to local heroes. At Hyde Park Corner, larger-than-life figures of bronze figures of gunners perpetuate the memory of 49,000 men of the Royal Regiment of Artillery who died in World War I. The animals which "fought" in two world wars are honoured in Park Lane. Britain's principal hero of World War II, Sir Winston Churchill, is an enormous, gruff-looking presence in Parliament Square. He appears again among the smart shops of Bond Street, sitting

The monument to Admiral Nelson was to have been even taller and grander, but the money ran out. Nevertheless, the 17 ft.-tall figure, sculpted by E.H. Baily in two pieces of Craigleith stone, tops out at 170 ft. The Albert Memorial is rich with reminders of the Consort's worthy inspirations. But hidden high in the canopy, sculptors furtively created some less chaste figures.

on a park bench, chatting to President Franklin D. Roosevelt – and there's space between them for a tourist to sit in on the conversation for a photo opportunity.

This is a more light-hearted tribute than most, for it was grief, official or heart-felt, at passings, and the heavy dignity of the church, that set styles and treatments. Thus Westminster Abbey, burial place of monarchs, remains the richest repository of sculpture in London, with some effigies surviving from the 13th century. But London's favourites are relatively recent: the high-Victorian kitsch of the Albert Memorial (1876) and the impish Eros in Piccadilly Circus (1893)

Prince Albert sits in a pinnacled pavilion among a melange of every memorial material of the time – marble, granite, bronze, mosaics, sandstone, limestone, slate, lead. Around the pedestal beneath him, 187 figures cut in high relief represent the arts and sciences that fascinated the Consort. Sir George Gilbert Scott's grand design in Kensington Gardens took 10 years to build and cost £120,000.

The cost of Eros was more problematical: it bankrupted the sculptor, Albert Gilbert, sending him into embarrassed exile. He was paid £3,000, but spent £10,000 – and was mocked for his efforts. The Establishment found it hard to accept that a memorial to a distinguished, aristocratic philanthropist, Lord Shaftesbury, should be a fountain for children to play in, topped by a naked boy symbolizing love. But Londoners did, indeed, love it, and it became their informal city emblem. Gilbert came home to be knighted 30 years later.

In the 1920s, Eros made this undignified exit from Piccadilly Circus so that the Underground station could be excavated. He spent the next several years in the Embankment Gardens – and then escaped the Blitz by being evacuated to Surrey.

It took half a century to work out how to get Cleopatra's Needle from Egypt to the Victoria Embankment. Finally, it was towed to London in a sea-going iron cylinder, a voyage that almost came to grief in a Bay of Biscay storm. The 180-ton obelisk was lifted into place in 1878.

SUFFRAGETTE LEADER
EMMELINE PANKHURST
VICTORIA TOWER GARDENS

PETER PAN
KENSINGTON
GARDENS

WAR MEMORIAL
HYDE PARK CORNER

HOLY CHILD JESUS
CAVENDISH SQUARE

THE WRESTLER
EMBANKMENT
GARDENS

ACHILLES
HYDE PARK

WILLIAM SHAKESPEARE
WESTMINSTER ABBEY

FAÇADE FIGURE
RIBA, PORTLAND PLACE

CELEBRATING TEMPERANCE
EMBANKMENT GARDENS

The Diana, Princess of Wales Memorial Fountain flows around an oval acre in Hyde Park. Water bounces down steps, sways through a sculpted channel into a babbling brook invigorated by bubbling jets, and slides over polished stones to rest in a reflecting pool. However, the American designer, Kathryn Gustafson, did not foresee the lack of respect from paddling dogs, London litterers and overly venturesome children: health and safety concerns have blighted its appeal.

The heroines of World War II had to wait longer for their memorial – 60 years. It was finally dedicated by the Queen in 2005. Near to the Cenotaph in Whitehall, the bronze by John W. Mills shows 17 sets of clothing – not just the uniforms of the 750,000 women who signed up for active service, but the outfits of ten times as many who served in the Land Army, as munitions workers and nursing volunteers.

KARL MARX
HIGHGATE CEMETERY

WORLD WAR I
MEMORIAL
HYDE PARK CORNER

THE UNKOWN BUILDER
BANKSIDE

OLIVER CROMWELL
PARLIAMENT SQUARE

THE WOMEN OF WORLD WAR II

ABRAHAM LINCOLN
PARLIAMENT SQUARE

CHARLIE CHAPLIN
LEICESTER SQUARE

SIR ROBERT SCOTT
WATERLOO PLACE

WAR MEMORIAL
CONGRESS HOUSE,
BLOOMSBURY

LONDON REGIMENT
MEMORIAL
ROYAL EXCHANGE

The Mall only assumed its full grandeur as a processional way as part of the tribute to the memory of Queen Victoria. Then Sir Aston Webb designed Admiralty Arch to mark the passage into Trafalgar Square.

A mounted Duke of Wellington originally topped Decimus Burton's Wellington Arch (left). Resited at Hyde Park Corner, Constitution Arch, as it became known, is now surmounted by Adrian Jones's quadriga – chariot and horses (main picture).

John Nash intended that the gateway to Buckingham Palace should be topped by a bronze equestrian statue of his patron, George IV. But the gateway, Marble Arch, impeded views, so it was moved to Oxford Street; the statue went to Trafalgar Square.

# Working capital

## INDUSTRIES

There were better places to build iron ships than beside the Thames. Nevertheless Isambard Kingdom Brunel commissioned *The Leviathan*, later called the *Great Eastern*, from the Scott Russell shipyard in Millwall. Brunel poses in front of the launching gear in 1857. In fact, it took six attempts and the death of a docker to get the 700-ft. long monster afloat.

There's little to show from the time when London was the most successful manufacturing centre in the country. Industrial archeologists may regret that, but if relics remained they would largely be reminders of grim conditions. Charles Dickens tells of that wretchedness, describing in *David Copperfield* the blacking factory beside Charing Cross where he worked as a boy.

Despite the pain, London was a hugely productive workshop. When ships were made of English oak, boatbuilding yards lined the downriver Thames. The 100,000 casual labourers who sought and fought for daily work in the docks unloaded raw materials that primed chemicals factories in Silvertown and Wandsworth, china production in Lambeth, furniture making in Bloomsbury. Huguenot and Jewish refugees stitched Londoners' clothes in Aldgate. And, of course, there were the breweries scattered across the city, dozens of them, which for several centuries provided the poor with the only potable form of Thames water.

As the industrial age took hold, London made a pitch for a share of the heavy work: railway locomotives were built in West Ham and Stratford, printing machines in Southwark. The standard British Army rifle for two world wars was made in Enfield, a little farther out, and bore the borough's name. But at the end of the Victorian era, the average London workforce was still less than 20 strong; thus the lack of grandiose remains – workrooms and sweatshops were tucked in wherever there was local demand for their output.

Thames Iron Works at Canning Town, connected to supplies of its materials by the Great Eastern Railway, continued building ships into the iron age, including a battleship in 1898 whose launch caused a disaster. The wave it created washed spectators to their deaths in the river. Warship construction moved north to more suitable waterways, the Clyde and the Tyne.

And this was a city with much else to do: a nation to govern, an empire to exploit, the world's banking to be audited, the new consumerism to be manipulated through advertising and marketing. These were more productive roles for an educated population and the capital's expensive locations than space-hungry manufacturing whose new-fangled assembly lines sprawled extravagantly across single-story sites.

Meanwhile, prosperous Londoners led the way into 20th-century consumerism, requiring the best of everything modern and modish. As early as 1892, the American Kodak company recognised their interest in photography. Kodak found cleaner air in which to make its sensitive products in Harrow, a little to the north-west. Serendipitously, it was a cheaper location offering a cheaper workforce, setting the style for London's continuing success in manufacturing. Between the wars, the north-western suburbs became the base for some of the proudest names in consumer products.

Back in the city, one flotilla of massive machines continued to reprise the noises that had mostly gone to the industrial north – the newspaper presses of Fleet Street whose nightly thunder was finally silenced in the 1980s.

# Wealth by water

## CANALS

Two miles downriver from London Bridge, among the wharves and warehouses of Limehouse, curved shoulders of pilings marked the entrance to an inland waterway of great potential. This was the Regent's Canal which opened in 1820 to connect the Port of London with middle England. Now, coals from Newcastle could fuel industries in the northern suburbs and imports from Empire could be unloaded in Birmingham from shallow-draft barges.

The country's canal system – in its prime, there were almost 4,000 miles of it – had skirted London out at Uxbridge, in Middlesex. In 1805, it reached Paddington through the Grand Junction Canal, later known as the Grand Union Canal. Pleasure

As late as the 1930s, North London's gas works received their coal supplies by steam-powered barge. By the 1950s, waterway imperatives had changed: the traffic became houseboats and pleasure craft visiting peaceful oases, one of which earned the soubriquet Little Venice (left).

boats made up much of the early traffic. Sun-starved Londoners, towed by "gaily-decorated horses," noted the "ruddy and healthful complexions of the cottagers' children" who spied on them from the cornfields.

The last link, the Regent's Canal extension, was less salubrious; there was a pastoral passage around Regent's Park, but then Camden Town, Islington, Hackney and Stepney lined its route. And while the freight-carrying barges carried payloads infinitely greater than could horse-drawn road wagons, they made slow progress: there were 12 locks between Paddington Basin and Limehouse to cope with an 84-ft. fall to river level.

The coming of the railways ensured that this was not to be a profitable investment (the Grand Surrey Canal leading through the southern suburbs fared even worse and was subsequently drained). But such is the appeal of a waterside location that the whole northern ring route remains a scene of constant urban renewal. The long-standing residential tranquillity around the pool at Little Venice in Maida Vale now abuts noisy construction at Paddington Basin, one of Europe's largest recent mixed developments. Apartment blocks and studios concentrate their glass-walled gaze on the narrow ribbon of water leading east from Islington.

Work in 1930s Stratford symbolizes confused ambivalence about the future of the Regent's Canal. A new wall is constructed so the waterway can be widened (left); nearby the canal is filled in (above) to the advantage of road traffic. The position soon became clear and further construction was usually to turn towpaths into pedestrian walkways.

# To the sea in ships

## LONDON DOCKS

Late 19th-century activity in what was then the world's largest port. One of the reasons for the port's sudden demise in the 1960s was the intransigence of union leaders with long memories of casually cruel employment practices, notably the hiring of dockers on a day-to-day basis.

The City jealously protected its interests, and one was control of trade passing through the world's most important port. Wharfing and warehousing around the Pool of London, between London Bridge and the Tower, was a money-spinning enterprise, but becoming absurdly inefficient. The capacity was 500 ships. Often there would be four times that number jostling for space, sometimes waiting weeks for lightermen to transfer cargoes to smaller boats and riverside wharves. Perishable food rotted; pilfering and plundering were lucrative local industries.

Finally, as the 19th century began, the great trading companies broke the City's stranglehold. A mile or so downriver was the long meander around the Isle of Dogs (named, it is said, for the royal kennels placed there, out of earshot of the palace at Greenwich). What if a canal cut across it, avoiding three miles of tedious navigation, where behind lock gates neutralising the tides, the booty of Empire could be unloaded directly on to quays and into warehouses, all behind secure walls?

The West India Docks opened in 1802; the East India Dock, downriver in

Blackwall, in 1806; the Surrey Dock in Rotherhithe a year later. The City regained a share of the action at St Katharine's Dock, hard by Tower Bridge. The man-made waterfront became one of the sites of London, "worth a detour," as the guidebooks say, for the towering redbrick warehouses built to handle trade that was worth £250 million in 1900.

The final development was the largest, most distant of all, an initiative of railway contractors who connected the facility to an efficient transport system requiring no passage through the costly, complex capital. Out on Plaistow Marshes, where the Thames could accept the deep drafts of the new iron ships, the Royal Group of Docks – Royal Albert, Royal Victoria, and the King George V Dock, completed much later, in 1921.

The runway of London City Airport is now the centrepiece of the lagoon here, where the 35,000-ton liner *Mauretania* eased in from Gallions Reach in the summer of 1939. The whole of Docklands is in a jerky process of regeneration. Warehouses make fashionable apartment blocks; wet docks are marinas. Modern container ships approach no closer than Tilbury, round just a gentle S-bend from the open sea.

Offloading cargo into smaller boats was still the practice in the 1870s (below) when scores of companies competed for the business, charging exorbitant fees and exploiting a labour force that was constantly topped up by needy and cheap immigrants. The Port of London Authority was formed in 1909 to bring order to the waterfront.

A cargo for India is manoeuvred by the London Mammoth floating crane (right). This 100-ton locomotive had been displayed at the 1951 Festival of Britain to promote pride in the "made in Britain" label.

The Greek Revival Euston Arch was revered as the monument to the railway age. Its demolition in 1962 alerted Londoners to the vandalism associated with rebuilding.
PHILIP HARDWICK, 1838

The grandest station frontage of all – the Midland Grand Hotel at St Pancras, towering over Euston Road. At journey's end, train drivers were encouraged to nudge the buffers as they stopped, to boost pressure in the hotel's hydraulic lift system.

# The end of the lines

### RAILWAY STATIONS

Railways were a British invention. The motive had been to carry the materials required by the Industrial Revolution more speedily than canal barges could, so the early network was freight-carrying, threading through the smoke-stacks of northern England, with the collieries as the departure points.

But London was a service city: the movement of people was the priority. In 1837, the first main-line railway terminus faced the city on its northern edge – Euston, named for the nursery gardens it replaced. A year later, the track reached Birmingham, 110 miles away, a five-hour journey, and this early demonstration of the way the railways could transform travel and fundamentally change the character of Britain was celebrated in style: the architect Philip Hardwick built a 72-ft. high portico on four huge Doric columns as the entrance to the station. Then came the Great Hall, a 62-ft. high Roman-Ionic concourse under a coffered ceiling.

Monumental and competitive station-building was under way. But the chaos and upheaval caused by installing railway infrastructure was quickly noticed, not least by Charles Dickens in *Dombey and Son*. As usual, it was the poorest of the poor who suffered. Middle class Londoners could use the very railway lines that displaced them

Victoria was two stations side by
side, occupied by two railway
companies. One served Brighton,
the other, Dover and the Continent
– routes made possible when the
first London railway bridge across
the Thames opened in 1860.

Unlike its ornate neighbour, St Pancras, King's Cross (top) was a no-frills exercise in engineering, with two great arches anchoring the train shed roofs behind. LEWIS CUBITT, 1852.

Charing Cross is the main line station closest to the centre of London. Like St Pancras, it is fronted by a hotel. The forecourt spire is a replica of the

Eleanor Cross, associated with the funeral route of Edward I's queen. All London distances are measured from it. JOHN HAWKSHAW, 1864. HOTEL: E.M. BARRY

Wrought iron, cast iron and glass compose "the gateway to the west" at Paddington Station (right). ISAMBARD KINGDOM BRUNEL, 1854

to move out to the suburbs; slum dwellers dragged their belongings a few streets away, adding to the overcrowding of their own kind.

Aristocrat landowners were having none of that on their London estates. So the great termini were kept out of town; London never boasted a "Grand Central," like New York. To the north, the line drawn was the New Road, later Euston Road. On it, to the east of Euston Station, came King's Cross (1850) and St Pancras (1866). Along the same meridian, to the west, is Brunel's Paddington Station (1856), and Marylebone (1899), the last mainline terminus built in London.

King's Cross was constructed without ornament, a functional place whose later glamour would derive from its *Flying Scotsman* service. St Pancras, on the other hand, flaunted the power and wealth of the railway barons. Its frontage is the huge Gothic hotel built by Sir George Gilbert Scott, raised high above the street to give the tracks behind a manageable incline over the Regent's Canal.

In fact, it was Londoners heading south and east who enjoyed the city's first steam passenger service – in 1836, from Bermondsey. Its success led to London

High, wide, and well-ventilated. The need to disperse the vapours of the age of steam gave London some vaulting interiors: decorated ironwork separates the aisles at Paddington (above, in 1910), and an uninterrupted 240-ft. wide, 100-ft. high arch at St Pancras (left, in 1958), was a marvel of Victorian engineering.

The modest concourse of Marylebone Station in the 1920s (right). The Great Central Railway spent so heavily on tunnels to avoid disturbing Lord's cricket ground and the wealthy enclave of St John's Wood that there was little money left to build the station. It was designed by a staff engineer, who took a bolts and braces approach.

H.W. BRADDOCK, 1899

Bridge Station. But these services stopped short of the river. Once that challenge was overcome, Victoria Station came to epitomise the promise of the railway age. Here, at the edge of fashionable Belgravia, was "the gateway to the continent," a title that would later go to Waterloo Station, whose much-admired International Terminal (Nicolas Grimshaw & Partners, 1993) gave Eurostar passengers a dramatic start to their journeys through the Channel Tunnel.

The five most westerly of Waterloo's 21 platforms were commandeered and lengthened for the Channel Tunnel rail link terminus, then covered in a giant, curving canopy of glass. This was one London infrastructure project that defied convention: it was completed months before the client was ready to use it.

A confusion of sheds and platforms made way for a new Waterloo Station in 1922. Its noble main entrance, now little-used, was designed by J. R. Scott as a memorial to railway staff killed in World War I.

A Postmodern take on the arched station roofs of old, with the lightness of slim steel chevrons framed by stone-faced towers. Embankment Place (left) sits on top of Charing Cross Station, a commercial development exploiting the station's air rights. Facing the river, it is a display of northern pride to south Londoners, outshining the South Bank show.

TERRY FARRELL & PARTNERS, 1991

# Spans and suspensions

## BRIDGES

Time and traffic overwhelmed both the original London Bridge (above) and its successor (below). For 300 years, it was the custom to display the tarred heads of traitors above the gatehouse of the former.

The bridge that nourishes Londoners' nostalgia, by way of prints on pub walls, calendars and Christmas cards, is one that pre-dates their experience by almost 200 years. It's a scene of countless arches, bulging with overhanging buildings, a church spire in the middle, peopled by cheerful cockneys trundling carts to market. It was the first stone bridge over the Thames, on almost the same site as its several wooden predecessors, all destroyed by fire or floodtides.

Those tiny arches were its undoing. Mills to pump water or grind corn filled many of them, leaving the few that were navigable as treacherous channels

regularly overwhelmed by the tides. "London Bridge was made for wise men to go over and fools to go under." Many an overturned boat proved the truth of that local adage.

Nevertheless, it served for 600 years, until the next London Bridge, with just five stone arches, designed by Sir John Rennie, opened in 1831. That one, deemed "the noblest on the Thames," finished up as a tourist attraction gracing a lake in Arizona. Now there is a pre-stressed concrete structure of three spans, completed in 1972.

Vested interests in the City and in Southwark, its southern landfall, profited handsomely from their control of the only river crossing. They managed to prevent the construction of a second until the middle of the 18th century. Then the Swiss engineer Charles Labelye built Westminster Bridge. The City/Southwark monopoly broken, London began to get the river crossings it needed, at Blackfriars (1769), another one to Southwark, at Waterloo, Vauxhall,

Collecting tolls at Putney Bridge in 1880. To protect London Bridge's toll income, the City of London had opposed the building of crossings closer than this one, high up the Thames.

Ferrymen controlled the river crossing at Fulham until Sir Joseph Ackworth's wooden bridge landed in front of Putney parish church in 1729. After 150 years of patching and petitioning – its 26 narrow spans seriously impeded river traffic – it was replaced by Sir Joseph Bazalgette's granite bridge, seen here being widened to allow for tram traffic.

Reaching the lively pleasure park across the river at Battersea was a trek for

Chelsea residents. They lobbied for a bridge, which was built in 1858, and lobbied again for pedestrian tolls to be waived on Sundays. Chelsea Bridge was strengthened more than once, but 20th-century traffic required its replacement (right). It took just four months to scrap the old bridge and make way for a new 83-ft. wide, four-lane crossing.
RENDEL, PALMER & TRITTON
with G. TOPHAM FORREST AND E.P.
WHEELER, 1934

Lambeth; further upriver, Battersea, Chelsea, the picturesque and complexly engineered Albert Bridge from Chelsea to Battersea, at Hammersmith and at Chiswick, and a renewal of the Putney bridge that was older than any of the more central crossings other than London Bridge.

The other iconic Thames crossing, Tower Bridge, between whose Gothic towers 1,000-ton bascules are raised still to allow tall ships entry to the Upper Pool of London, opened in 1894. It is the only city bridge not to have been rebuilt or replaced as traffic pressures rose. Labelye's Westminster Bridge, for instance, made way for Thomas Page's cast-iron structure in 1862.

Finally, Tower Bridge arises
to serve bustling East
London without hindering
tall ship traffic to the Upper
Pool. Anchored by massive
piers in the river bed, its
11,000 tons of steel were
clad in Portland stone and
Cornish granite, in a style
in keeping with that of the
nearby Tower. Londoners
came by boat to see it
opened by the Prince of
Wales.
SIR JOHN WOLFE BARRY,
SIR HORACE JONES, 1894

The drawbridge, the largest of its day and still in regular use, was first powered by steam engines which could raise the bascules in less than a minute. The high walkways, served by lifts, have now been glassed in.

The first new London bridges for a century are both devoted to pedestrians, and both lead to the cultural attractions of the South Bank and Bankside. The Jubilee Walkways are suspended on either side of a Victorian eyesore, the Hungerford railway bridge, which serves Charing Cross Station.
LIFSCHUTZ DAVIDSON, 2002

An innovation known as lateral suspension allowed the Millennium Bridge to cross the Thames without the need for tall support towers that would have concealed St Paul's. But the slender structure wobbled under its opening day traffic; £5 million spent on shock absorbers and dampers brought stability.
FOSTER & PARTNERS, OVE ARUP & PARTNERS, 2000

"Every drop of the
Thames is liquid 'istory."

JOHN BURNS, LEADER OF THE
LONDON DOCKERS' UNION.

Sir Joseph Bazalgette, the top-hatted figure holding the plans (left), close to the end of his city-saving project, where the three northern sewer pipes approach the Abbey Mills pumping station. Londoners still depend on Bazalgette's sewer system of the 1860s; the underground photograph, (below right) shows maintenance work in the 1950s.

Bazalgette's achievement ended in a monumental flourish – the Byzantine pumping station at Abbey Mills in East London (above). Giant beam engines occupied an equally ornate interior. There is now more modern pumping equipment nearby, concealed under a gleaming aluminium "barn."

# Mains and drains

## WATER AND WASTE

The world's first and greatest metropolis was shamefully tardy in providing its citizens with clean running water and seemly sewage disposal. Manhattan piped in crystal clear torrents via the Croton Aqueduct in 1842, but it took frequent outbreaks of cholera and the "Great Stink" of 1858, when Parliament had to seal its windows against the stench of the Thames, before London seriously addressed the issue – which was the river itself, principal source of its water and the cesspool for its sewage.

Water provision at that time was a private enterprise (which it would revert to being in 1989). Eight hugely profitable companies dug up the streets at random, just as the utility companies do now, to lay pipes, first of bored-out elm trunks, later of lead, to bring water to those who could afford it. Most of it came from the Thames, some from the River Lea to the east, from the springs of Hampstead and Highgate, more from a purpose-dug, 40-mile canal, the "New River", from Hertfordshire to a reservoir in Islington, an imaginative 17th-century project. In the background, the Honourable Company of Water Tankard Bearers, churlishly eager to preserve their back-breaking trade, lobbied against the provision of running water.

One water company's claim that its supplies were clean was based on the boast that the river water in its reservoirs was allowed to settle for 24 hours before it was distributed. In 1829, the Chelsea Waterworks Company introduced "slow-sand filtration." The poor, whose floorboards were often laid across open sewers, used standpipes that might be primed for less than an hour a day.

In the 1850s, more than 80 members of Parliament were shareholders in London's water companies, not anxious for the common good to erode their dividends. But outrage was mounting and in 1852, the Metropolis Water Act ruled that the water companies must tap into the river above Teddington Lock, the barrier against tidally-carried sewage. Slowly and reluctantly, the suppliers responded, but it was not until 1902 that the Metropolitan Water Board took over the private companies and the public interest became the paramount concern.

And the river flowing through London had to be cleaned up so that travellers crossing the bridges need not put scented handkerchiefs to their noses. The engineer Sir Joseph Bazalgette devised the plan. The 60 main outlets disgorging into the Thames were rerouted into five cavernous brick sewers, three north of the river, two on the south side, and, assisted by great steam pumps, their contents dumped in lagoons at Barking and Erith, to be released into the river on the ebb tide. By 1887, a chemical precipitation process was working to separate solids from liquids so that they could be barged out into the North Sea.

London and its hinterland now has a "ring of water," a tunnel sometimes 65 metres below ground, supplying 8 million people with water cleaned at three treatment plants. The dead river is once again home to fish.

# Cutting the corner

## VICTORIA EMBANKMENT

The Thames would have been half a mile wide where the Roman intruders disembarked. To the north, they would have seen a wall of dense woodland; to the south, where Southwark now stands, a less defined margin, as the tide lapped uncertainly over mudflats and marshes, sand and gravel banks.

But this lazy river became the key to London's prosperity. It was controlled and contained. The accoutrements of shipping – docks, wharves, and warehouses – acquired firm footings at the water's edge, barriers between the citizens and their greatest natural amenity. By Victorian times, however, commerce was moving downriver to new docks dug out of the banks. Even the slips and landings for ferries were falling into disuse as new bridges made the boatmen redundant. And to the west of the declining activity was a stagnant shoreline that disgraced the world's greatest city.

It was time, and here was the place, for London to have a worthy waterfront. An idea that Sir Christopher Wren had put forward 200 years before, a grand riverside terrace, was fulfilled by Sir Joseph Bazalgette, Chief Engineer to the Metropolitan Board of Works.

The Victoria Embankment, known to Londoners now just as The Embankment, stretches from Westminster Bridge to Blackfriars, underlining the old Palace of Westminster, rounding the curve at Charing Cross, fronting the lawns of the Temple Inns. Bazalgette built out into the river, reclaiming almost 40 acres of land. Steam pile-drivers mounted on barges drove in the containing outline; brick walls faced with granite rose above cement foundations. And, buried beneath it all is the true object of the exercise, Bazalgette's greatest contribution to London's welfare: a massive drain to intercept and carry away eastwards the sewage that made the Thames a stinking cesspool.

By 1868, Londoners had a stretch of riverfront to call their own. A broad, tree-lined carriageway, gas lights atop lamp posts encircled by intertwined dolphins, and benches for promenaders supported by sphinxes and camels. Cleopatra's Needle was lifted into place for their admiration in 1878; Queen Boudicca and daughters, cast in bronze, in 1902; cast-iron dragons from the City in the 1960s.

And Bazalgette had been busy elsewhere giving the metropolitan Thames a crisper outline. He laid out the Albert Embankment south of the river, then the handsome Chelsea Embankment, where he again took the opportunity to divert sewage from the river. Soon each of these public amenities was overwhelmed by traffic. Riverside promenading now is along the South Bank's pedestrian precinct, among the "string of cultural pearls" between Westminster Bridge and Borough Market.

An elegant new promenade and an easy connection between London's power bases – the City and Westminster. As well as housing the drain that cleansed the pestiferous river, the Victoria Embankment covered the tracks of the Metropolitan District Railway.

# Providing the energy

## POWER STATIONS

Two chimneys, then three, then four, as Battersea Power Station grew to serve London's appetite for energy. It opened in 1933, was completed 20 years later, and allowed to sink into dereliction 30 years after that. It is a heritage-listed building, but efforts to revive it for public use have been hampered by the menace of its asbestos content and the sulphur absorption into the fabric that enabled its vapour emissions to be comfortably white. The turbine hall (above) had the calm order to be expected of the church architect who designed it.

Lighting and heating London became a competition between two new sources of power that appeared in the 19th century. There were gaslights on Pall Mall in 1807; on Westminster Bridge and in the Haymarket Theatre in 1813. Thomas Edison built the first electricity power station at Holborn Viaduct in 1878, illuminating the Old Bailey and the General Post Office. The new Savoy Theatre was the first to be electrically lit, in 1881.

Gas was much, much cheaper to make; its delivery relatively simple. It took a long while for the electricians to choose between direct current and alternating current, and to decide on a practical voltage level. Early DC supplies were carried short distances – no more than a mile, on overhead wires that were liable to overheating – from local, privately owned generators.

Gas became a domestic fuel in the 1890s, and soon even the poorest households were cooking by it, buying a penny's worth at a time through pre-payment meters. Electricity was proving its worth as a clean power source for trams and underground railways.

Manufacturing both fuels required vast quantities of coal, and cooling water. Gas was made in plants along the River Lea and the Regent's Canal. The Gas Light and Coke Company, which was assuming dominance in a fiercely competitive

Sir Giles Gilbert Scott also designed Bankside Power Station, after World War II. It was planted deep in the Southwark soil and had just one "inconspicuous" chimney, in deference to St Paul's Cathedral's presence across the river. The building became the Tate Modern gallery, with help from the Millennium Lottery Fund.

business, built a gasworks at Barking Creek, beside the Thames. This was Beckton, named for the head of the company. It became the world's largest coal-fired gasworks, supplying London through 48-in. diameter pipes, storing its supplies in the telescopic gasholders that became as ubiquitous to Londoners as church steeples. Beckton closed in 1976, having served London for a century.

Electricity supplies, and suppliers, proved more difficult to rationalize. In 1914, more than a dozen companies were digging up the streets to lay cables from 70 generating stations. Local government intervention brought some sense to it: a major unifying power station at Barking (1925), and at Battersea, where the architect Sir Giles Gilbert Scott built the lasting London industrial landmark (1933).

# Down the tubes

## THE UNDERGROUND

Refining Brunel's tunnel-boring technique, James Greathead devised a cutting shield behind which circular segments of cast iron lined and secured the bores, as at the work in progress (above) on extending the Central Line to Liverpool Street in 1912. Compared with New York subway tunnelers who faced bedrock, London's diggers had an easy time, through a 400-ft thick bed of clay. Nevertheless, such tunnelling was costing around £400,000 a mile in 1910 – almost £20 million in today's terms. Greathead's system was still in use lining an access shaft in 1932 (far right) and to get to work on the new Victoria Line in 1964 (below), the first new route in 60 years.

By 1855, 750,000 workers were converging on the city centre every day. They walked to work, or boarded the horse-drawn omnibuses that clattered uncomfortably along the cobbled streets. The river was thronged with ferries and some commuters arrived by train, on local services from Greenwich and Blackwall. But it was the immediate and roaring success of the Metropolitan Railway service from Paddington to Farringdon Street, by way of Euston and St Pancras, that transformed London's transport system. In 1863, its first year, 10 million passengers coughed and spluttered behind smoking steam trains traversing intermittent tunnels.

Cattle grazing the fields between Hyde Park and Notting Hill made way for commuter homes within reach of the service. Soon there was a line from South Kensington to Westminster, then services from Hammersmith and Swiss Cottage to Aldgate. By 1885, the distant northern villages of Pinner and Rickmansworth were prime commuter locations, at the edge of "Metroland."

Early tunnels were constructed by "cut and cover". Streets were dug up, a brick tube built, the track laid and the roadway replaced, with air vents discreetly reaching the surface (to this day, there are two faux house frontages in a Bayswater street behind which the old locomotives let off steam, and smoke). Routes underlining roads avoided easement payments to the owners of properties that might be undermined, but it soon became obvious that if the metropolis was to be properly served, the network would have to go its own ways. Tunnels would need to be bored, and – new thinking – electrification would overcome the problem of smoke.

There was an engineering precedent. Sir Marc Isambard Brunel, father of the more famous engineer, had built the world's first underwater tunnel intended for public transport below the Thames, from Rotherhithe to Wapping, in 1843. It was a dark and

dank tube that never appealed to Londoners, but the methodology – inspired, it was said, by the way shipworms bored into wood – was proven.

The modern Underground network spread under the City, the West End, the inner boroughs. Trains approached the platforms up an incline, to help slow them, and departed down an incline, to aid acceleration.

Suburban communities had first attached themselves to the spokes made by the old Roman roads, such as Watling Street and the Old Kent Road. Now the

Underground served the spaces in between. Where the tracks surfaced – more than half the 250 route miles are overground – house-builders were waiting, and they bought land where they thought the lines might go. Estate agents set up sales huts in open fields alongside the tracklayers, empowering the house-building boom that followed World War I.

As the Underground reached out into new territories, there were sometimes no rail links to put its rolling stock in place. Thus a carriage intended for the new service starting at Morden, a village in Surrey, is manoeuvred through suburban streets in 1926. Fives years later Morden's population had increased tenfold.

## STATEMENT STATIONS

Frank Pick, the visionary head of London Underground in the 1920s, did not take it for granted that business would be brisk; he had a service to sell to the public. He commissioned travel-promoting posters that are now considered classics of graphic design, inspired typography for nameplates and notices that immediately established an identity, and, most dramatically, encouraged a school of public architecture that created some of the metropolis's most iconic buildings – notably stations that grace the Piccadilly Line, Arnos Grove and Southgate, Sudbury Town and Hanger Lane.

Pick's eager partner was Charles Holden, of the Adams, Holden & Pearson architectural partnership. Holden's first assignment was to remodel older stations whose style was that of the domestic dwellings around them (indeed, the stationmaster's house was often the most significant feature). Thereafter, his original thinking led to landmarks on bland suburban high streets.

Mindful that, down the line, passengers would be plunged into noisy darkness, that journey's end would be claustrophobic caverns under Piccadilly Circus or the Bank, Holden welcomed them into extravagant spaces: high, light and airy ticket halls where a morning paper and a packet of cigarettes could be bought for distraction on the commute – and a late-opening florist's shop sold bouquets to celebrate the wage-earner's return.

Pick and Holden toured the continent to learn Modernist design lessons, in Scandinavia particularly. They rejected as overwrought the curvaceous Art Nouveau embellishment of the Paris Metro and the pseudo-Tsarist splendour of Moscow's subway system. Instead, they went for surfaces of undisguised reinforced concrete and steel, boldly curved and geometrically angled, to frame high, wide windows whose internal illumination advertised the stations at night. Outside, the service's distinguishing emblem, a bull's eye crossed with the keyword, mannered as UNDERGROUND, stood high on a mast or tower.

At first, 50-passenger lifts carried travellers to the deep-level platforms. At one station-opening ceremony, the Prince of Wales wondered aloud whether he was going down in the world, or it was going up. By 1913, escalators were the specified conveyances, and soon assumed the airy, comforting formula of these at Leicester Square, with the signature uplighters. The three-escalator format here allowed for rush-hour flexibility.

# STOPS ON THE LINE

The London subway system began with each line a separate commercial fiefdom. Among the more powerful players was an American, Charles Tyson Yerkes, who understood that appearances mattered; his architect, Leslie Green, established the early identity with red, glazed-tile exteriors that sloughed off grime and rain, and Arts-and-Crafts features to the booking halls. As the Underground system coalesced, Frank Pick and Charles Holden continued to pursue a unified visual and practical presence – but with an open-mindedness that moved with, and often ahead of, the times. More than one of their 1930s showcase stations was planted "in the middle of nowhere." Communities grew around them.

CANTILEVERED CANOPIES AT ARNOS GROVE.

ALDGATE EAST – FOR ACCESS TO ESSEX.

WANSTEAD – A FLORAL WELCOME FOR COMMUTERS.

AN EXPERIMENTAL CONCOURSE AT GANTS HILL IN 1947.

ARNOS GROVE – A NEW SHAPE FOR 1932.

PARK ROYAL'S TOWER – A MARKER FOR A NEW SUBURB.

The Jubilee Line extension headed out through Docklands by way of a series of dramatic new stations commissioned by the architect-in-chief, Roland Paoletti. At Canary Wharf (below), the builders anchored a 985-ft.-long concrete box in the waterlogged earth of a former dock. Inside, they built the station under an elliptical glass canopy that takes light to every corner of the concourse.
FOSTER & PARTNERS, 1999

At the eastern end, the Jubilee Line connects with older services under Stratford's new glazed roof (right) – the rejuvenation of a station first built in 1839 for "the capital of the East End."
WILKINSON EYRE, 1999

Welcoming Jubilee Line commuters by getting natural light into the depths was a design preoccupation at the new stations – by way of curved glass walling at Canada Water (above), refracting fins at Southwark (left), and cobalt blue glass reflecting through perforated metal at North Greenwich (far left).

CANADA WATER: ROLAND PAOLETTI AND JLE ARCHITECTS, 2000
SOUTHWARK: MACCORMAC JAMIESON PRICHARD, 2000
NORTH GREENWICH: ALSOP, LYALL & STORMER, 2000

# London flies

## AIRPORTS

The first Englishman to gain a pilot's licence built himself an aerodrome in North London – albeit in the days when a mown grass strip served the purpose. Claude Grahame-White bought a 200-acre estate in Hendon and from 1911 used it as a base for flying displays which the RAF continued between the wars. Original buildings there survive as part of the RAF Museum.

For a while, Hendon had the title London Aerodrome, but there were other contenders to be the city's main airport. Hendon had been on the wrong side of town

A Handley Page Hannibal Class HP42, Imperial Airways' flight from Croydon to Paris, prepares for departure on a winter evening in 1937. Checking-in was a relaxed affair (above).

to fend off German airship and aircraft attacks in World War I, so Croydon Aerodrome, to the south-east opened in 1915. By 1920 it had customs facilities for international travellers.

Meanwhile, an airfield a little east of present-day Heathrow was making a bid for traffic; there was a daily London-Paris service from Hounslow Heath in 1919. The first flight to Australia took off from here in November of that year. There was other flying from London bases – Northolt, still used for royal and governmental flights, and Kenley and Biggin Hill, honourably remembered now for Battle of Britain heroics – but Heathrow was chosen as the capital's berth for the expected post-war boom in civil aviation. What started as a tented city in 1946 has been a building site ever since, as every forecast of likely traffic has been overwhelmed by actuality. The world's busiest international airport is presently building its fifth terminal, a space designed by the Richard Rogers Partnership to process 30 million passengers a year under a 68,000 sq.m. glass roof.

In 1939, Imperial Airways opened an Art Deco terminal beside Victoria Station (above left), from where a rail link took passengers to the flying boat base at Southampton. The canopy statuary represents "Speed Wings Over the World."
A. LAKEMAN

In 1956, watching planes go by was
still thought of as a glamorous
accompaniment to dining;
Heathrow catered for the voyeurs
in its new Queen's Building
(above), set between the parallel
main runways (opposite below
in 1978).

London City Airport opened for routine
business commuting to Europe's
financial centres in 1987, promising
shortened check-in times rather than
starched linen service. The water-
flanked runway is built on the quay
between the old King George V and
Royal Albert Docks.

London has a stolport (short take-off and landing) for the quiet and nimble jets and turbo-props that can manage the steep descent across the City on to a Docklands runway. But the overflow of conventional traffic is absorbed well outside the metropolitan limits, principally at London Gatwick and London Stansted. Like Heathrow, Gatwick has experienced forced growth, fitting in facilities when and how it could. Only Stansted had the pre-prep time to plan a merit-worthy architectural statement – Foster & Partners' single-story terminal, which, in 1991, quadrupled the airport's passenger capacity, to 8 million a year.

Tall tubular steel "trees" of 50 ft.
support the Stansted terminal's roof,
conceal its air conditioning and
uplighting and, nearer the floor,
house flight information monitors and
safety equipment.

Gatwick's configuration – two far-
apart terminals and a single runway
– required much bussing of
passengers to aircraft. A 656-ft. long
passenger bridge (above, right) now
links the North Terminal to a
satellite, reducing bus traffic on the
taxiway below. So as not to disrupt
aircraft movements, the bridge was
prefabricated a mile away, ferried to
the site and hoisted into position.
WILKINSON EYRE, 2004

Terminal 5, latest and largest stage in the never-ending building programme at Heathrow. When completed with planned satellite buildings, it will have stands for 60 aircraft, some designed to take the Airbus A380 "superjumbo" whose wingspan is 80 metres. If Terminal 5 were a stand-alone airport, it would be the fourth largest in Europe.

# Keeping moving

## ROADS

Londoners were fretting about congested streets 500 years ago, but perhaps the apogee of atrophy was mid-Victorian times when almost everything that moved in the now vastly-busier capital still did so by road. Wagons and drays, hansom cabs and hackneys, omnibuses and coaches fought for right of way among the smoke of millions of coal fires and the emissions of 200,000 working horses.

It had all begun promisingly: the lasting mark of Roman colonization is a road system, and London's was particularly neat. Traffic still follows the paths of four great highways, roughly north, east, south and west, that carried Roman rule to Lincoln and York, Colchester and St Albans, Canterbury and Dover, Bath and Gloucester. Later London streets just attached themselves to that frame of arteries. Further streets and alleys spread between them, ingeniously providing frontages for houses and workshops, taverns and stables. By medieval times, there was gridlock.

After the Great Fire, Sir Christopher Wren proposed a boulevard-based layout to anchor the rebuilding. Landowners thwarted his vision, allowing only that there should be a minimum street width of 14 feet in the rebuilt City. And now there was a larger London to negotiate, unstructured, growing all the time, engulfing villages and settlements in every direction.

Nash carved the first north-south highway through the city centre. This triumphal route, Regent Street (1823), reached towards the New Road, from Paddington to Islington, which was thought to be the city's northern perimeter

Resurfacing Whitehall amid a street party atmosphere, around 1910 (above). A night-time drive through east London offered a selection of surfaces (left). Early materials were mud and cobbles, to be packed down by the traffic – or rutted by it, depending on the weather.

Then broken stones bedded in sand or gravel, followed by brick-sized granite setts, and locally-fired bricks made to a non-slip formula; cobblestones treated with coal tar, pitch and creosote oil; concrete macadam and tar macadam; wooden roads: deal blocks and planks saturated in boiling tar with pebbles between the joints – a quiet ride this, but prone to wear; harder woods – Australian eucalyptus, American red-gum – but these were slippery. London tried them all, including a rubber roadway to the Savoy Hotel entrance, so that the noise of carriage wheels would not disturb the guests. Threadneedle Street, in the City, was the first (1869) to be paved with asphalt – crushed stone and bitumen. That would be the long-term winner.

"My Lord of Ely, when I was last in Holborn, I saw good strawberries in your garden there..."

WILLIAM SHAKESPEARE,
*RICHARD III*

when it opened in 1756. Certainly, it acted as buffers when the railways approached, but development quickly leaped over it.

New Oxford Street, at St Giles, and Commercial Street, Spitalfields, eased long-standing bottlenecks on ancient routes, and served the additional purpose of razing slums – as did Victoria Street, which cleansed the ghetto west of Westminster Abbey. But affordable space was running out. Since Charing Cross Road and Shaftesbury Avenue completed the West End's street pattern in 1886, and the broad thoroughfares of Kingsway and the Aldwych took some strain off the Strand (1905), road builders have hardly laid a finger on central London.

But they still had work to do in Greater London. Bridge and tunnel-building had opened up the south where the principal landowners, the Church, more readily made space for roads than the estate owners north of the river. After World War I, the highway authorities gained new land-purchasing powers and arterial roads reached out in all directions. New communities anchored themselves, limpet-like, to these tentacles – "ribbon development." Then there had to be by-passes so that long-established high streets were not overwhelmed by thundering through-traffic.

Wishful thinking by urban planners, begun in the 1930s, emerged again after World War II. The overloaded local roads of Hackney and Hampstead, Battersea and Lewisham could be returned to the people if they would just find room for radials and ringways. But Londoners would have none of it. At planning inquiries in the 1970s, they raised 20,000 objections. The distant, orbital M25 was one of the few projects to survive their scrutiny. And the elevated Westway, at the end of the highway from Oxford, was allowed to step into town, placing one of its giant feet in the churchyard of St Mary's, Paddington Green.

When the over-bearing Westway bludgeoned a path across communities in Paddington and North Kensington in 1970, Londoners pledged "never again." At this point in its construction, the old White City stadium, the Olympic venue of 1908, still stands – top left of the photograph.

# Spreading out

## THE SUBURBS

In simpler times, key workers lived over the shop – bakers above their ovens, cobblers over their lasts, dressmakers over their fitting rooms. But there were dirtier trades to accommodate: butchering, brewing, candle-making among many. Those London citizens who could afford to moved away from the noisome environment, to the west, upwind of the smells. And as the making of bread and boots and beer became functions of production lines in factories outside the centre, the workers, too, could disperse. Furthermore, at the apogee of Empire, there was a new shabby but respectable calling that became the main occupation of central London: perched on their city office stools, thousands of clerks kept the account books of Britain's global trade, scratching copper-plate handwriting into leather-bound ledgers.

Where were these people to live, and take advantage of the freshly-minted thinking that each new, child-bearing generation should be independent home-makers, liberated from parents and grandparents? In a process that had begun modestly in the 17th century, urban sprawl gathered momentum. In 1800 there had been 1 million Londoners; by 1900 there were almost 7 million, locally administered by 28 metropolitan boroughs.

Landowners were persuaded that there was more money to be made from building than farming; the dairy farms between Hyde Park and Notting Hill filled with modest homes. The Metropolitan Railway's Paddington to Farringdon Street service (1863) delivered clerks to their desks. As the London Underground's network spread, villages on both sides of the river, Islington and Kilburn, Camberwell and Kennington, were subsumed into a sea of bricks made from the clay that was London's own subsoil.

Managers and professionals aspired to detached "villas;" lesser wage-owners started out close-packed in terraced houses, whose earliest configuration was a front parlour alongside a hallway leading to the kitchen and the outside privy, with two bedrooms above. Few architects were involved; there were pattern books to follow, and minimal building standards.

Mostly, these homes were rented by their occupants from the builders, whose

Ilford in Essex was an early dormitory suburb, primed by an effective rail service. The 1930s dual carriageway indicates the future; the neat front gardens would soon become off-street parking.

## FULFILLING THE SUBURBAN DREAM OF SECURITY AND RESPECTABILITY: STYLE

FROM VICTORIAN TIMES TO THE 1930s FOR UPWARDLY MOBILE LONDONERS

source of credit was the building societies which first appeared in the 1850s, and would later come to finance the nation's home ownership. (The ownership of freeholds, a social ambition more prevalent in Britain than in many other advanced countries, was encouraged by Freehold Land Societies, whose motive was to increase the number of voters at a time when the franchise was restricted to freeholders.)

London's house-building boom only came to a halt under the barrages of World War II. By this time, prefabricated construction processes requiring less-skilled labour were filling the dwindling greenfield sites and lining the sides of the new arterial roads with respectable suburban homes, semi-detached more often than not, that took just three weeks to build. Three bedrooms, one bathroom, a kitchen, two living rooms, space for an asbestos garage alongside – £500, with a mortgage of less than £1 a week.

Wembley was burgeoning around its new stadium, stirring development of the nearby village of Kingsbury; from there a little-used train line headed north across open land. So, next stop Queensbury, where 50,000 homes were built in the 1930s (left). After the war, many more homes were needed – and teenagers had to be taught to build them (below).

Selling the suburban dream at 1930s homes exhibitions. The delight, it was thought, was in the details: a tile-hung bay, prominent chimneys, leaded windows with a hint of stained glass, a rustic wall to the miniscule front garden – echoes of cottages and vernacular traditions And where to build the real thing? Choose a place name on Beck's map of the Underground, whose distorted geography suggested that the greenfield sites of Hendon and Highgate were just a hop away from the workplaces in Holborn.

# Local livelihoods

## SUBURBAN INDUSTRY

The flight to the suburbs gained impetus from a road-building programme officially sponsored to ease post-World War I unemployment. Arteries leading west were among the most extravagant projects – the Great West Road and the Western Avenue, now tributaries of the M4 and M40.

For the planners, the roads were the thing; what might line them was left to developers. Multi-national companies took up station, their buildings making power statements to the passing traffic. Communities filled the gaps – in the 30s, the notion of living on a main road had a trendy appeal – and here were the new enterprises' work forces. Residents of the agreeable ribbon developments were eager to work locally rather than commute, the tedious alternative destiny.

Their activity was serving London's consumer market, making cosmetics and cookers, toothpaste and tyres. The production lines are long gone, but several of the attention-seeking buildings remain. A supermarket now lurks behind the Hoover frontage, but this dignified, Modernist face still earns respectful glances from motorists hurrying along the Western Avenue toward Oxford.

The Gillette factory's clock tower was the landmark emblem of the Great West Road's "golden mile" of industry where London's status as a manufacturing centre was maintained between the wars.
SIR BANISTER FLETCHER, 1936

By 1938, Londoners owned 500,000 cars; Trico made windscreen wipers for them. The nearby Firestone factory on the Great West Road kept them in tyres. Thought to be the finest of the neighbourhood's buildings, it was demolished in 1980, leading to public outcry and campaigns to preserve its contemporaries.

Thomas Wallis, architect of many respected buildings on the western approaches, aimed "to bring dignity to the workplace." Certainly the frontages achieved that. He set an Art Deco "altar" over the Hoover building's front door (above) and indicated moated surrounds to the Coty (cosmetics) and Pyrene (fire extinguisher) factories (far right). More orthodox detailing greeted visitors to the Maclean's toothpaste business (right). Such buildings now bear other logos; warehousing is their usual role.

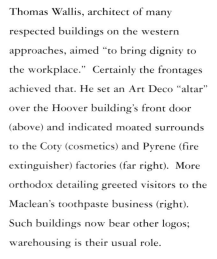

"The first thing to do," said Psmith, "is to ascertain that such a place as Clapham Common really exists. One has heard of it, of course. But has its existence ever been proved? I think not."

P. G. WODEHOUSE, *MIKE*

# Living in layers

## APARTMENT BLOCKS

Maida Vale, named for an Italian battlefield where a British force defeated the French in 1806, was church land north of Paddington, west of the Roman Watling Street. The Church Commissioners controlled its development caringly, around broad avenues of fine houses and terraces, and later, Edwardian mansion blocks such as these in Wymering Road (above and right).

There was a need for bachelor pads or, as the Georgians put it, residential chambers for gentlemen – comfortable, serviced quarters for men about town and country squires requiring a part-time address amid the city's affairs and its fleshpots. It began elegantly, at Albany, a conversion, in 1802, of Lord Melbourne's Piccadilly townhouse, but it was half a century before the first mansion block of flats was built.

Parisians had long lived like this, and it was becoming the New York style, although, in an unlikely burst of Yankee snobbery, a commentator wrote, "no gentleman will live on a mere shelf under a common roof." London's doubts about these tall machines for living rested on their threat to privacy – to be damaged, surely, by overlooking windows; by dislike of the shadows they would cast; and the fear that they might just sink into the London clay.

The opportunity to test such shibboleths arose on Victoria Street, a long, straight, wide thoroughfare built to clear the slums west of Westminster Abbey, a road to Pimlico that nobody knew quite what to do with. The city's first mansion block appeared here, in 1853. Then Artillery Mansions, three six-story blocks, European in style, under Dutch gables, with bathrooms, wine cellars and passenger lifts. Soon red brick monoliths filled the area – Evelyn Mansions in Carlisle Place (1893), Albert Mansions, Ashley Gardens – putting young bureaucrats within walking distance of their Whitehall offices, their clubs, and Victoria Station, the departure point for weekend getaways to Brighton.

Some were splendid, like Whitehall Court, an 8-story French Renaissance block built on the Victoria Embankment; another, Queen Anne's Mansions, reached a height of 180 ft, causing such outrage that the planning laws were revised.

Once the association of flats with tenements was banished from middle-class minds, families found in the mansion blocks an agreeable, affordable way to live close to the city's lively heart. The idea transplanted to Kensington where Norman Shaw built the enormous Albert Hall Mansions in 1879. Blocks appeared in Marylebone and Knightsbridge. Pretty villas on the north side of Regent's Park were replaced by luxury high-density.

Great houses with grand addresses made way for flats, such as the Duke of Portland's home in Grosvenor Square. And even in the villa-laden suburbs, flat-dwelling became modish, and sometimes architecturally exciting, as in Lubetkin's 1930s Highpoint development overlooking the city from the heights of Highgate. Here, the Swiss French visionary Le Corbusier, who admired few architects' work other than his own, expressed approval – "a vertical garden city."

Curiously, it was back close to Victoria beside the Thames where the most confident of all pre-war speculations in flats was made: Dolphin Square (1937), the largest self-contained block in Europe at the time, is home to 1,250 tenants in bland slabs spread over 7.5 acres.

After World War II, Victoria Street, where it had all begun, renewed itself as an enclave of office blocks. The riverfront became the prime location for living in layers, as disused docklands warehouses were converted into highly-prized, high-ceilinged, wide-open studio apartments. This encouraged developers to move upriver, toward Battersea and Chelsea, building blocks where penthouse prices clicked up to seven figures; and downriver, to Canary Wharf, where the skyscraper architects Skidmore, Owings and Merrill will be topping out Pan Peninsular at 500 ft. There are to be 820 apartments on 50 floors. Suggested prices here reach eight figures. A parking space is £30,000 extra.

A vast World War II bomb site gave the City the opportunity to welcome back residents after centuries of population decline. In the 1950s work began on the Barbican – 2,000 housing units in an inward-looking enclave. This "good address" has never been short of tenants, but neither has it been viewed with affection. The concept – the landmark high rises (these were planned as the tallest residential buildings in Europe) punctuating high-density blocks clothed in reinforced concrete and connected by secure, but bleak walkways – is now viewed as one of the wrong turnings taken by post-war urban planners. A barbican was a medieval city fortification; this one seemed to repulse life around it.

CHAMBERLIN, POWELL & BON, 1973

A showcase for curves at Bankside Lofts,
beside Tate Modern in Southwark – in
the lift- and stair-tower and roof bracing
(left), and a tower of apartments (above)
with glazed exteriors to single- and
double-height spaces. An old cocoa mill
is at the heart of the development,
where residents acquired shells to fit out
as they pleased.
CZWG ARCHITECTS, 1998

Even Chelsea had its downtrodden, war-ravaged areas. The Royal Borough cleared one of them to build the World's End Estate, between the fashionable King's Road and prime river frontage.
ERIC LYONS, CADBURY-BROWN, METCALF AND CUNNINGHAM, 1977

A less congenial outlook in North Paddington (below). Fire damage to tower blocks here at the Elgin Estate revealed the asbestos used in their construction.
LCC ARCHITECTS' DEPARTMENT

In the 1930s, the Russian-born architect Berthold Lubetkin built some of London's most admired Modernist buildings. He believed that architecture should be a means of social renewal; his Tecton practice was given this public housing commission, in Islington, in 1949.

founded by Sir Edward Guinness began building for the urban poor in 1890; again, Guinness is still a London address, on much-modernized estates. But it was the London County Council that would have the greatest impact, becoming in time the city's largest landlord: by World War II it had built 90,000 homes for renting.

Formed in 1888, the LCC collected wide powers, to use in co-operation with the 28 metropolitan boroughs. Its remit would come to include main drainage, building controls, parks, welfare, education and public health. And it began with a social conscience. The Housing of the Working Classes Branch was staffed by young architects committed to the egalitarianism preached by the Fabian socialists, and devoted to the honest quality pursued by the Arts and Crafts movement.

Their first project was a 14-acre site in Bethnal Green that had been cleared of a rookery known as the Nichol. By 1898, streets radiating from a central garden, complete with bandstand, were lined with five-story blocks of flats – a thousand families had kitchens and toilets, and schools and shops nearby. The conundrum, though, remained: few of the Nichol's displaced persons, lucky to earn £1 a week, could afford the rents. They melted into other slums.

That happened again at Millbank, where a huge old prison made way for Sir Henry Tate's gift of a gallery for British art and an LCC housing estate, and at other worthy inner city projects. The economics were intractable. The LCC turned to the small print of its remit: it had the power to compulsorily purchase land for working-class housing, and it did so where it was cheaper, in Tooting and Tottenham, Camberwell and Croydon. Publicly-funded "cottage estates" stirred the housing and social mix of the suburbs.

This enlightened programme continued until World War II, but even then there was still much slum clearance to do. Hitler's Luftwaffe assisted, brutally, in the fire bomb Blitz that began in September, 1940. The East End took the brunt of it, accounting for a large part of the 300,000 London homes deemed damaged or destroyed. The post-war rebuild took another approach to the land cost problem: high rises, tower blocks of flats, a concept encouraged by government subsidies and the city's inability to spread any further: it was bounded now by the Green Belt, a band of countryside officially protected from development.

By the end of the 1960s, the view across the city from Hampstead Heath was punctuated by more than 400 angular monsters, mostly ugly, quick to peel and corrode in the polluted air. Certainly, they fitted in more residents to the acre, but not as humanely as those early, enlightened LCC architects would have wished. A new planning mantra followed: "low-rise, high-density."

In Brunswick Street, Hackney, housing association tenants emerged from the post-war shadows to pay £1 a week rent for flats whose balconies were aligned to receive at least half the day's sunshine (left).

Tenants of Southwark prefabs – the immediate response to the bombing of London's housing stock – have their futures behind them as the Brandon Estate arises in 1959 (right). Nine years later, the gas explosion that collapsed a corner of Ronan Point in Newham ended the planners' infatuation with tower blocks (far right).

The Peabody Trust moves with the times: a forbidding housing block built to last in Pimlico; and experimental accommodations in Southwark, designed as short-term, affordable housing for key workers, in this case, nurses. Barons Place used off-site modular construction and took just 14 weeks to erect; it can be dismantled and rebuilt if there is more pressing need elsewhere.

In the 1970s, Camden Borough architects found a way to stay low and yet achieve the maximum permissible population density of 210 people an acre: the Alexandra Road estate is cantilevered out over railway tracks.

The concrete blocks of Kensal House in North Kensington (below, left) were notable in their day for the modern efficiency of their cooking and heating systems; the development was on a site owned by the Gas Light and Coke Company.
MAXWELL FRY, 1936

East London marshland was blotted dry to make way for the GLC's admired Thamesmead housing project. But it used a feature that planners later learned to avoid: walkways that filled with litter and became menacing places after dark.

A pit stop at Piccadilly Circus in the
1890s (right), and a bolder approach
at Notting Hill (main picture), where
the local amenities group
commissioned "the Turquoise
Island."
CZWG ARCHITECTS, 1992.

# Relief at the roadside

## PUBLIC TOILETS

There were flushing toilets for visitors to the Great Exhibition of 1851 – one of the wonders of the event – though the inventor of the devices, George Jennings, seemed strangely discomforted in marketing the idea: he called them "monkey closets." But until Joseph Bazalgette installed London's 1,000 miles of main drains, there was little opportunity for discreet and hygienic relief in public places.

The first properly flushed public toilet, for men only, appears to have been in Fleet Street, a precinct remarkable for the incidence of pubs and taverns. Soon such places became a ubiquitous feature of the Victorian city: an underground cavern marked by tall railings, a lamp-lit stairway under a curved iron arch, polished brass handrails, glazed white tiles.

Women in need had longer to wait; it was considered immodest for them to publicly acknowledge a call of nature. Not until 1884 were they able to "spend a penny," the price to use the Ladies' Lavatory Company's new facility at Oxford Circus.

Boys only at this entrance to the Hugh Myddelton school in Clerkenwell, one of the turn-of-the-20th century schools that, by 1904, were giving free education to 750,000 London children.

The notice boards promote evening classes for senior students, the deaf, and stammerers. Hugh Myddelton founded the New River Company which brought clean water to the area

in the 17th century. The school has since been demolished. And girls only at Kidbrooke Comprehensive, the first school purpose-built (1954) for the new system of secondary education.

# First classes

## SCHOOLS

Once they were persuaded that the economy could survive without the cheap toil of 10-year-olds, the Victorians took to building schools as if the future depended on it – which, of course, it did. Literacy and numeracy were required of the workforce now, not just raw energy and nimble fingers. Following the Compulsory Education Act of 1870, youngsters were drilled in the 3Rs in imposing, tall-windowed blocks set alongside churches and chapels and on the new housing estates. By the 1920s, the London County Council was operating 1,000 free elementary and secondary schools across its region, staffed by 24,000 teachers.

The better-off had, of course, always been better educated, though some of their more elitist and venerable schools had started with charitable intent. St Paul's School, twice rebuilt beside the cathedral before moving out of the City, provided free education for 150 boys as early as the 16th century. The actor-manager, Edward Alleyn, set up almshouses and a school for "six poor scholars" in 1605. It is now Dulwich College, housed in an Italianate block built by Charles Barry, son of the architect of the Houses of Parliament. At Harrow School, equally expensive and prestigious, there's the whole history of school-building in evidence, from a schoolhouse of 1615 to modern science laboratories.

In the run-down north London
neighbourhood of Harlesden, the
youngest children may get their first
school experience in the bright context
of the Fawood Children's Centre. They
are introduced to computers in a
Mongolian-style tent, and play in "the
deepest sandpit in the borough."
ALSOP DESIGN, 2002

Pimlico Comprehensive won an
architectural award but was not so
popular with pupils, who found the
hothouse effect of the glazing
uncomfortable.
GLC ARCHITECTS, 1970.

A modern take on the cloisters of
Oxbridge at the Capital City Academy in
Brent, a metal and glass rebuild of a
former secondary school.
FOSTER & PARTNERS, 2003

# Higher learning

## UNIVERSITIES

Senate House (right) opened as the tallest building in the country – London's first true skyscraper. According to the city's folklore, Hitler earmarked it to be the Nazi headquarters after his conquest of Britain; but some say the choice was Whiteley's department store, in Bayswater. George Orwell, too, thought Senate House gave an ominous impression: the Ministry of Truth in his novel *1984* is modelled on it.

The century-old system of higher, vocational education at Polytechnic colleges was consolidated in the 1970s with central London served by a new building on Marylebone Road (below). It later became part of the University of Westminster.

The tall tower of Senate House looms over Bloomsbury, the city's academic quarter. But even from this 210 ft. high vantage point, much of collegiate London's "campus" is beyond distant horizons. Out at the fringes of Greater London, there's Thames Valley University in the west, the University of East London in Docklands; Middlesex University north of Hampstead, and the magnificent Surrey mansion where the Royal Holloway College was one of the first for women. And then there's a muddle of 40 or so other sources of higher education dotted between them.

Senate House was built in the 1930s as the University of London's headquarters. The architect was Charles Holden, best known for his Underground stations, and here, his sparse classicism is grandly displayed in Cornish granite and Portland Stone, clothing gleaming travertine interiors. Holden planned a spreading complex in the style of Senate House, but World War II intervened.

The original academic building, University College (1829) presents an earlier version of classicism to Gower Street, but, in the absence of Holden's grand design, the university has colonized the surrounding area in a haphazard way, often offending admirers of Bloomsbury's Georgian heritage. And the college's original charter – a dedication to educating non-Anglicans – so offended the Archbishop of Canterbury that he sponsored King's College, which opened in 1831 beside Somerset House. The two combined as the University of London (Senate House is named for the senate of eminences who conducted the degree examinations) which has been absorbing other colleges, such as the London School of Economics, ever since.

Just as South Kensington vied with Bloomsbury to be the capital's museum focus, so it set out to have an academic presence in the wake of the 1851 Great Exhibition. Over there, the emphasis was in line with Prince Albert's devotion to learning that had commercial application. Thus, Imperial College, to encourage technology, and the Royal College of Art, devoted, in part, to industrial design.

The concentration of museums and colleges in South Kensington is known as Albertopolis, in tribute to Prince Albert's ambitions for the precinct. Foster & Partners worked on a 1990s masterplan to rejuvenate the area; some of their open-plan ideas have been put into practice at Imperial College (below).

London Metropolitan University's London North campus opened a new Graduate Centre in 2004 (left and above) built by Daniel Libeskind in typically angular mode.

# Power to the people

### TOWN HALLS

Bustling Battersea's administrative allegiance was once to the leafy county of Surrey; deprived Deptford's to hop-growing Kent. With the creation of the London County Council in 1889, such communities were finally properly identified – as working components of the capital city. Local governance now resided in 28 metropolitan boroughs, with the LCC overseeing the services that concerned them all – policing, transport, regional development. The boroughs built town halls, grand Victorian and Edwardian statements of authority, but none was as grand as the headquarters that the LCC planned for itself, and finally occupied in 1922.

As late as the turn of the 20th century, the view across the river from the prim new Victoria Embankment was of decaying workshops and rotting wharves, a wasted waterfront in a prime position alongside Westminster Bridge. The LCC took the site. The only major commission of a young architect, Ralph Knott, who died before the project was completed, County Hall rose in "Edwardian Renaissance" style, Portland stone on a granite base that matched the new river wall.

It served the LCC and its successor authority, the Greater London Council, which the Thatcher government, outraged by its Socialist leanings, abolished in 1986. County Hall was sold to a Japanese company for activities commercial rather than civic, and London went on to elect a mayor – who turned out to be Ken Livingstone, the GLC leader Thatcher had deposed. Livingstone's administration commissioned a new City Hall, a squashed glass globe with impeccable "green" credentials.

# Health and healing

## HOSPITALS

**Celestial and Terrestrial globes mark the entrance to the palatial complex at Greenwich that became the Royal Naval Hospital and, later, the Royal Naval College.**

**Pushed out of its original Southwark site to make way for London Bridge Station, St Thomas's Hospital used the compensation money to start a grand rebuilding best viewed from Westminster Bridge. The block pattern followed European practice at the time. Heavily bombed in World War II, St Thomas's has since been rebuilt yet again.**
**HENRY CURREY, 1871**

The humanity of the Church and private philanthropy provided London's sick beds until well into the 19th century, when tax money empowered a public hospital system. Augustinian canons built St Bartholomew's (Bart's), in West Smithfield, in 1123. It's still there, flaunting a few shafts of the original among a jumble of later building that includes Georgian grandeur. And to this day, London's most cherished hospital, the Great Ormond Street Hospital for Sick Children, benefits from a private endowment: Sir James Barrie gave it the copyright in *Peter Pan;* its reconstruction in the 1930s owed much to those royalties.

Containing infectious disease was the first concern of early hospitals. Leprosy was greatly feared until the 17th century, and London had eight or more "lock" hospitals, as they were known, including St James's, which would become a royal palace. Other leper hospitals came to cope with the diseases spread by prostitutes and filthy drinking water. The quarantine zones around them were quickly overwhelmed by the growing city and, as modern medicine reduced the risk of epidemics, they settled into being generalized facilities.

Important among the teaching hospitals was University College Hospital, opened in 1837 when the new University of London required a medical school to challenge the Oxford and Cambridge monopoly on awarding degrees in medicine. Florence Nightingale trained nurses at St Thomas's, whose beginnings were even earlier than Bart's: it is a massive modern presence (1980) across the river from the Palace of Westminster. And near London Bridge, Guy's, the first London hospital to teach dentistry, has added tower blocks to the handsome frontage of 1722.

Eminent architects were among the enlightened citizens concerned for the well-being of the poor, and they often donated their services to these charitable projects. The design challenge was to indicate the safe isolation of disease within blocks of brick and stone, and yet signify the prestige of their patrons. There was benificence, too, for fallen heroes: Sir Christopher Wren, his pupil, Hawksmoor, and Sir John Vanbrugh all contributed to the Royal Hospital for military veterans in Chelsea, and the Royal Naval Hospital at Greenwich.

A new surgery unit arises at Guy's Hospital in the 1950s. The original building (top right) dates from 1726, endowed out of the fortune Thomas Guy made in South Sea stock trading. Activities at University College Hospital (left) befitted its role as a teaching hospital: the first European use of ether as an anaesthetic happened here. The nation's war veterans convalesced in grand surroundings – the Chelsea Hospital and the Royal Naval Hospital at Greenwich (right). Nelson's funeral procession passed along this stretch of river.

The Institute of Cell and Molecular Science at Queen Mary's School of Medicine and Dentistry in Whitechapel is designed for "world-class biomedical research" in an open plan environment. The openness extends to encouraging local schoolchildren to understand the programme: the giant orange molecule is the centre of an interactive learning facility.
ALSOP ARCHITECTS, 2004

Police vehicles dominated traffic at University College Hospital (below) in July, 2005, when it was at the centre of London terrorist attacks. Mothers and babies are the prime concerns behind the curved glass frontage of the Golden Jubilee Wing of King's College Hospital in south London (bottom).

# Beaming down

## BT TOWER

Built to do a job, the BT Tower certainly expresses function before form; its architects eschewed the pursuit of elegance that characterizes, for instance, Toronto's CN Tower, which serves the same purpose. The job is transmitting telephone and broadcasting signals, and behind the glass curtain-walling of most of its 620 ft. height (it can be 8 in. taller on a hot day) is the activity of endlessly updating communications systems which began there with electro-magnetic cabling.

For 15 years, this was the tallest building in London (yet still just a third the height of Toronto's tower). The designers noted that only circular buildings survived the blast waves of Hiroshima and Nagasaki, so the BT Tower, built during the Cold War, is round. This unmissable landmark was at first an "official secret" in bureaucratic-speak, not to be photographed, not marked on Ordnance Survey maps.

Nuclear-resistant it may be, but a bomb planted in a toilet in 1971 halted the eager flow of visitors. The tower was closed to the public for ever, and soon afterwards the revolving restaurant on the 34th floor was decommissioned. The perceived vulnerability up there perhaps relates to the fact that the only access is by two high-speed lifts. British Telecom's corporate guests, however, continue to enjoy the spectacular views on the 20-minute rotation.

The priority assignment of the Post Office Tower, as it was originally named, was to ensure radio connection with the country bunker where the Cabinet might survive a Cold War nuclear attack.
ERIC BEDFORD,
G. R. YEATS, 1965

# Protecting a capital

## DEFENCE, LAW, AND ORDER

Londoners hope that the forest of antennae and satellite dishes bedecking the MI6 building at Vauxhall Cross is to give them adequate warning of hostile forces – even though a dissident mortar fired from just across the street punctured its fabric and its pride in 2000.

Army barracks provide more traditional reassurance, and they occupy prestigious London addresses – Wellington, across the road from Buckingham Palace; Chelsea, at the southern edge of Sloane Ranger territory; and Knightsbridge, bordering Hyde Park. All three have long histories at those sites; all three have been reconstructed in recent times, and now Chelsea is in the sights of commercial developers.

Wellington and Chelsea are long, low structures, necessarily large, but unobtrusively styled. Knightsbridge Barracks, where there are almost as many of the Queen's horses in residence as men, has a more belligerent look. Its 328-ft. high concrete tower, built in 1970 by Sir Basil Spence, has the unhappy distinction of being the one close building to rise above the tree canopy when looking south from the heart of the park. Out at Woolwich, on London's eastern frontier, the 1,050-ft.

There was once a garrison town behind the triumphal white entrance to Woolwich Barracks (top). "Old" New Scotland Yard also had a grand entrance archway; Brixton Prison's was more forbidding. A Brigade of Guards regimental crest identifies the residents of Chelsea Barracks (opposite).

frontage of the Royal Artillery Barracks (1802) is the city's longest architectural composition, and a handsome one at that.

The original need for garrisons close to the heart of town had much to do with fear of the enemy within — civil unrest. Now, that concern is the province of the Metropolitan Police. Bobbies first stepped out on the beat in 1829, from Scotland Yard, in Whitehall. As the century progressed and the bobbies' relevance and respectability grew, the Victorians began building police stations across the capital.

"Tudor-Gothic" was the early "default" style, but eminent architects contributed more singular works, such as Norman Shaw's three-story, yellow brick station house in Kentish Town. Fire stations, too, added to reassurance in the increasingly orderly city — 26 were built in just five years (1867–71) by the Metropolitan Fire Brigade's own architect, Edward Cresy. A later facility that remains in service near Euston Station is an eye-catching reminder of the Arts and Crafts movement.

**Knightsbridge Barracks**, a closed citadel on the southern edge of Hyde Park occupied by the sovereign's ceremonial cavalry. T. H. Wyatt's building was demolished in the 1960s.

MI6, the most furtive of the security agencies, operates from this hardly-discreet concrete and green-glass fortress. It was intended that there should be an apartment block here, but Prime Minister Thatcher commandeered the site for her spies. The design retained the homely features of bows and balconies overlooking the river.
TERRY FARRELL & **PARTNERS, 1993**

The Metropolitan Police commandeered not a site but a speculative build, two metal and stone slabs in Victoria Street, and named it New Scotland Yard. It should be New New Scotland Yard, to distinguish it from the previous headquarters on the Embankment.
CHAPMAN TAYLOR **PARTNERS, 1966**

Scaffolding arises from the centenary cleaning of the Albert Hall in 1970 (right). On the frieze encircling the building, dejected warriors acknowledge "the triumph of the arts and sciences". A steam engine originally powered the 10,000-pipe, 150-ton organ (above).

Behind the first-floor colonnade of the Queen's Hall (below), Henry Wood devoted 60 years to popularizing serious music. In its early days as a "musick house," Sadler's Wells in Islington attracted audiences in an earthier fashion: a pint of porter was included in the ticket price. Dance is the fare at the latest – the fifth – theatre on the site (below right).

# Making music

## CONCERT HALLS

London was always a musical city. The cacophony of street musicians – organ-grinders, bagpipers, drummers – was often noted by 18th century diarists, and at a more refined level, there was performance to rank with the best of Vienna and Milan. The young Handel and the child prodigy Mozart played for London audiences. Playgoers were accustomed to musical intermissions at the theatre. Concerts at the lively pleasure gardens of Vauxhall and Ranelagh in Chelsea delighted royals and their humble subjects.

For the 50 years up to World War II, the city's musical heart was Queen's Hall, in Langham Place, at the northern end of Regent Street – a classical Italianate exterior enclosing a comforting Victorian interior of gilding and red plush. Here, in 1895, Henry Wood launched the Promenade Concerts that are still the populist highlight of the musical year. Queen's Hall was bombed to rubble in 1941, and the Proms moved to the Royal Albert Hall – though it was not until tinkering in the 1960s that its acoustics pleased the purists (one eminent conductor had earlier said, "the Albert Hall can be used for a hundred things, but music isn't one of them").

Sir Henry Cole, responsible for spending the profits of the 1851 Great Exhibition on cultural institutions to be built around Kensington, distrusted architects, so this great brick oval supporting an iron and glass dome 135 feet above the auditorium, was designed by two army engineers. Wagner conducted concerts here in 1877 and, ever since, the Albert Hall has played a key role in the musical life of London.

For purer sound, there is the Wigmore Hall, a more intimate setting not far from the Queen's Hall site. It was built in 1901 as the Bechstein Hall by the German piano maker of that name, next door to his London showroom. The name was changed in 1917 in the wave of anti-German feeling. After World War II, new musical venues arose in the South Bank complex, and at the Barbican in the City, where the concert hall is considered one of the better features of that unruly development.

Covent Garden is the shrine for disciples of ballet and opera. Behind its six massive Corinthian columns dominating Bow Street, the Royal Opera House of 1858 entered the 21st century with a massive make-over partially and controversially funded by the National Lottery.

Covent Garden's neglected Floral Hall alongside the Royal Opera House (left) became a glamorous feature of the complex in the 1980s/90s renovation, which included restoring the sparkle of the richly-decorated auditorium and providing backstage facilities worthy of a world-class national opera house. The architect of both buildings was E. M. Barry. His was the third theatre on the site; fires destroyed its predecessors. The recent renewal agitated Londoners, who questioned the spending of Lottery money on what was perceived to be an elitist interest.

GMW ARCHITECTS, 2000

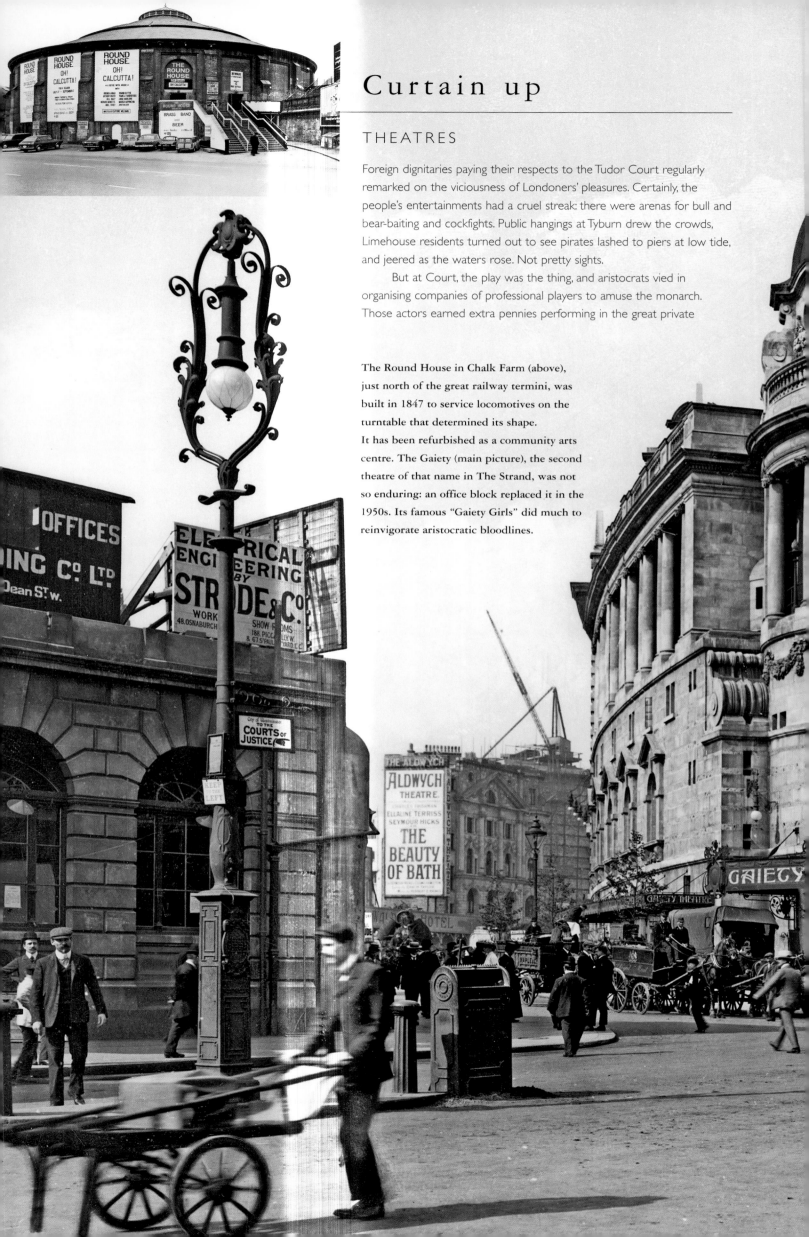

# Curtain up

## THEATRES

Foreign dignitaries paying their respects to the Tudor Court regularly remarked on the viciousness of Londoners' pleasures. Certainly, the people's entertainments had a cruel streak: there were arenas for bull and bear-baiting and cockfights. Public hangings at Tyburn drew the crowds, Limehouse residents turned out to see pirates lashed to piers at low tide, and jeered as the waters rose. Not pretty sights.

But at Court, the play was the thing, and aristocrats vied in organising companies of professional players to amuse the monarch. Those actors earned extra pennies performing in the great private

The Round House in Chalk Farm (above), just north of the great railway termini, was built in 1847 to service locomotives on the turntable that determined its shape. It has been refurbished as a community arts centre. The Gaiety (main picture), the second theatre of that name in The Strand, was not so enduring: an office block replaced it in the 1950s. Its famous "Gaiety Girls" did much to reinvigorate aristocratic bloodlines.

houses and in the courtyards of inns, and it was one of them, James
Burbage, who in 1576 created in Shoreditch the first purpose-built theatre,
where a paying audience gathered around a platform on trestles. When the
lease expired, Burbage and his company – which included William
Shakespeare – pulled down the Theatre and rebuilt it on Bankside, as the
Globe, alongside a bear pit.

Theatres were discouraged in the City itself: the authorities
considered them hotbeds of licentiousness. The Globe was one of several

The theatre in the Haymarket had a reputation for unruliness and a habit of troubling the censor, the Lord Chamberlain. When Nash was asked to rebuild it, he chose a site next door, so that this handsome Corinthian-columned portico could be seen from his new boulevard, Regent Street.
JOHN NASH, 1821

Shaftesbury Avenue, London's last new thoroughfare, opened in 1886. Side-by-side theatres, all built on the northern frontage of the street, quickly earned it the title, "the heart of theatreland."

"… the eyes of men,
After a well-graced actor
leaves the stage,
Are idly bent on him
that enters next."

SHAKESPEARE, *RICHARD II*

across the river, outside the jurisdiction. Others were built in Blackfriars, including the Dorset Garden Theatre (1671) whose classical façade, attributed to Wren, faced the Thames. It had the form of a modern theatre, with the stage framed by a proscenium and the means to change scenery sets.

By the middle of the 18th century, Londoners were committed though rowdy theatre-goers. At the Theatre Royal, Drury Lane, the actor-manager David Garrick was truly a celebrity. But the theatres of the time were prone to burning down – the footlights were wicks in bowls of tallow – and theatres such as Garrick's made several appearances under the same name; the present Theatre Royal is the fourth.

London's other Theatre Royal, in Haymarket, was perhaps the first act in London's rise to being the world's premier theatre city. In the later 19th century, the actor-manager Squire Bancroft replaced the pit where an unruly crowd gathered with stalls seating, banishing the "pitties" and so allowing closer attention to the comedies of manners that were becoming the favoured fare. Sir Herbert Beerbohm Tree built Her Majesty's Theatre across from the Haymarket (1897). The Savoy (1881) staged Gilbert and Sullivan operas under electric lighting, the first London theatre to have it. The Shaftesbury (1888) was the first of six theatres built in Shaftesbury Avenue in just 20 years. A night "up west," as Edwardian Londoners put it, offered a choice of 40 theatres.

The actor Sam Wanamaker devoted his last years to building a replica of Shakespeare's Globe (top), a few yards from the site of the original. Old records dictated the materials: lime plaster over oak laths, hand-made bricks, and thatching of Norfolk reed. The Alhambra in Leicester Square (above) awaits the demolition crew in 1936; it had been one of the late 19th-century's most-loved music halls.
GLOBE: THEO CROSBY, 1997
ALHAMBRA: PERRY & REED, 1883

# WHERE THE SHOWS GO ON

Audiences from the train-served suburbs, less fear of fire as electricity replaced open-flame stage lighting, the entrepreneurial egos of actor-managers, sophisticated new plays by Pinero and Oscar Wilde… the stage was set for the Victorian and Edwardian impresarios.

THE PALACE, CAMBRIDGE CIRCUS, BUILT TO BE AN OPERA HOUSE.
G.H. HOLLOWAY, T.E. COLCUTT, 1891

THE CRITERION, PICCADILLY CIRCUS. THE BASEMENT THEATRE WAS SECONDARY TO A RESTAURANT IN THE GREAT PROSPERITY, 1874

THE VICTORIA PALACE BILLING THE CRAZY GANG AS THE HEADLINE ATTRACTION. FRANK MATCHAM, 1911

THE ALDWYCH THEATRE WAS REBUILT SEVERAL TIMES BEFORE AND SINCE THIS VERSION OF THE EARLY 1900s

A HEAVY FRONTAGE FOR FROTH AND LEGERDEMAIN AT THE LONDON PALLADIUM. FRANK MATCHAM, 1910

THE VAUDEVILLE THEATRE IN THE STRAND, BUILT IN 1870, REMODELLED 20 YEARS LATER.

A hint of the Empire State Building in Kilburn High Road where the Gaumont State proclaimed itself "The World's Greatest Theatre." Inside, audiences of up to 4,000 passed through a marble-columned, mirror-lined foyer to a "Renaissance" auditorium.
GEORGE COLES, 1937

Strictly modernist Art Deco at the Coronet, Woolwich (below), built in 1937, now a church; and Cubist zigzags and stylized clouds frame the cashier at the Regal, Marble Arch. Unlike theatres, cinemas tended to place the box office right at the front door; thus the need for weather protection.

# Settings for the silver screen

## CINEMAS

Every kind of popular entertainment had been staged at the Empire Theatre, Leicester Square – ballet and burlesque, operettas, revues, musical comedies. In among them, one evening in 1896, a new kind of show flickered across an empty stage – a projected cinematic film made by the French photographer Auguste Lumière.

Twenty years later London had 100 "picture palaces" or "electric theatres." They were modest, boxy rooms: impresarios were not yet convinced that Londoners would forego their much-loved music halls for this new-fangled entertainment, silent except for a lonely piano. But the logistics were so simple – need only for a canvas screen, a projector and rolls of film (highly flammable though they were) – that shows featuring the most famous faces of the day could be profitably presented in the suburbs.

Once "talking pictures" and Technicolor established the medium, national chains of film distributors hired specialist architects to give cinemas a style of their own. Regals and Rialtos, Odeons and Gaumonts became dominant buildings on the high streets of

Wandsworth and Stepney, Fulham and Brixton, rivalling the Underground stations with their clean, modern lines.

The opulence was on the inside, where the steeply-raked seating of an amphitheatre might be contained in dragon-bestrewed Chinese splendour or a fantasy Moorish palace under an Arabian Night projected on to the ceiling. Adding to the cultural confusion, the console of a mighty Wurlitzer organ, vivid in ivory and gold and with an organist costumed to match, rose from the pit to provide orchestral overtures and, at the touch of a button, to indicate the mood of the movie to come through clanging sleigh bells, clattering horses' hooves or deafening decibels of dawn chorus.

In 1935, the Trocadero at Elephant and Castle opened as the biggest cinema in Europe, seating 5,000. The Empire, Leicester Square, where it had all begun, continued as a theatre until 1927. Then it was demolished and the Empire Cinema took its place.

Either side of the fluted verticals in Portland stone, there are horizontal bands of windows and spandrels – an unembellished continental style fresh to London in 1930. The New Victoria was a breakthrough in cinema design in other ways, notably in that the stalls seating was below ground level so that filmgoers looked up at the screen. Close-set fluting continued in the foyer;

the auditorium was themed as a "mermaid's palace." Pale green lighting glinted off mother-of-pearl effects on the walls; wave and shell patterns adorned carpets and upholstery. The New Victoria remains in show business, now as the Apollo Victoria Theatre. It was one of the first cinemas to gain heritage-listed status.
E. WALMSLEY LEWIS, 1930.

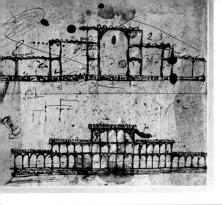

# Raising glass for a celebration

## THE CRYSTAL PALACE

Photographs from the 1850s show how closely the final building followed Paxton's first blotting paper doodle. Hothouse plantings at Sydenham indicate the inspiration for his design.

It was a "marvel of the age," yet its inspiration was a country greenhouse. It disappeared 70 years ago, yet its image is instantly recognizable. Its prime time was just 150 days, yet its nickname lives on as a South London address.

From May to October 1851, the Crystal Palace occupied 19 acres of Hyde Park as the showground for the Great Exhibition. Prince Albert was the driving force for this thoroughly worldly celebration, where the humble crafts of distant colonies would be juxtaposed with the highest technological achievements of the age. But how to house it?

Joseph Paxton, the Duke of Devonshire's consultant gardener, had proudly realized a glass lily house on the estate at Chatsworth. He

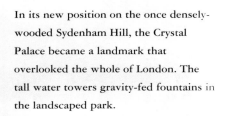

In its new position on the once densely-wooded Sydenham Hill, the Crystal Palace became a landmark that overlooked the whole of London. The tall water towers gravity-fed fountains in the landscaped park.

scaled up the drawings and with the power and patronage of the Consort behind him, won the design competition. In four months, 2,000 workmen bolted together that iconic shape, 1,848 ft. long, 408 ft. wide, with its signature arched transept 108 ft. high, added so that three large elm trees did not have to be cut down. Prefabricated panels used 4,000 tons of iron, 400 tons of glass.

There were misgivings about the structural integrity. Platoons of soldiers were marched up and down the corridors; cannon balls rolled around the wooden aisles. But all was well. Six million visitors, rajahs and their retinues, provincial farmers making their first journies on the new train services, and the Duke of Wellington who, it is said, walked over from Apsley House almost every day, came to admire Prince Albert's vision of the best of times.

Its purpose served, the Crystal Palace was deconstructed as quickly as it had gone up. It reappeared on Sydenham Hill in South London greatly enlarged, for a productive life as the heart of a recreation complex, served by its own railway station. In 1936, the wooden floors were its undoing: hothouse dry, they spread a small fire into a conflagration of melting iron and exploding glass.

Achieving the spare simplicity of slender
spars and glazing was first a matter of
complex scaffolding.

Leisurely labour on the Dome of
Discovery. Despite material
shortages and trade union disputes,
the world's largest domed building
took shape here.

# A preview of the future

## THE FESTIVAL OF BRITAIN

It was a big question for traditionally-minded, austerity-straitened Londoners: is this the future you want? At the 1951 Festival of Britain, on a blitzed and bedraggled river frontage at Lambeth, strange and disconcerting shapes suggested a way forward for their city.

Startling those accustomed to the sturdy stone of South Kensington's Victorian museums, the main exhibition hall, where tribute was paid to the nation's recent inventiveness – penicillin, radar, jet engines – was a vast upturned saucer of aluminium, the Dome of Discovery, whose supporting structure was nakedly exposed. The site's centrepiece, the Skylon, soared to almost 330 ft. as a slim, tapered shaft braced by wires – without a comforting flying buttress anywhere. And hereabouts was the kind of statuary that public patronage would be encouraged to sponsor in future: not lifelike heroes on horseback but semi-abstract distortions by Henry Moore and Barbara Hepworth.

The Festival set out to turn a page in the story of Britain's architecture and art. The team of architects led by Hugh Casson spoke of Modernism and Le Corbusier's vision of cities as machines for living. Under the auspices of the Welfare State, bomb sites and left-over Victorian slums were to be reborn in brightly-coloured, streamlined forms: festival visitors could get the idea at a model housing estate constructed for the occasion in nearby Poplar. They learned of the satellite new towns being built to relieve urban overcrowding and replicate, at greater distance, the Metroland suburbanization of the pre-war generation.

Londoners, still clutching their food ration books, still sifting through the wreckage of one war while sending their sons to another in Korea, took a truculent view of these promised lands. It was all very worthy, but they preferred the cosy confusion they had been born to.

Ninety-eight ft. high and spanning 394 ft., the Dome of Discovery dominated the 27-acre site. The Festival's rallying theme was Britishness, so the curved roof at the centre right of the photograph below proudly covers the Lion and Unicorn Pavilion in that most patriotic of materials, English oak. The Skylon hovered over the waterfront. Critics of the Festival's cost to the impoverished nation – and there were many – included Winston Churchill, who said of the Skylon: "It has no visible means of support – rather like the British economy."
DOME OF DISCOVERY: RALPH TUBBS
SKYLON: POWELL & MOYA

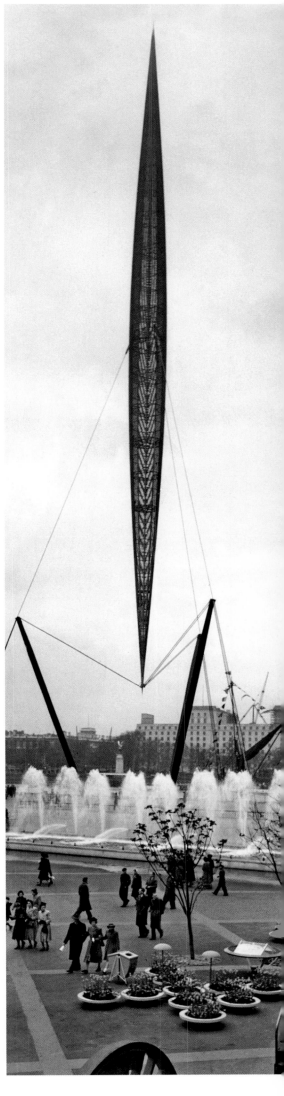

The Royal Festival Hall has been the calm centrepiece of half a century of distracted development on the South Bank. Its auditorium boxes (below), "like an open chest of drawers," were part of the pursuit of perfect acoustics.
SIR ROBERT MATTHEW, SIR LESLIE MARTIN, 1951

# Riverside reclamation

## THE SOUTH BANK

As the Festival of Britain complex was deconstructed, the promise that the London Thames would never return to being "a river with only one bank" had to be fulfilled. The Royal Festival Hall – still widely judged to be the city's best post-war public building – was firmly in place; a decidedly less majestic cultural ghetto arose beside it. The architects of the Queen Elizabeth Hall, the Purcell Room, the Hayward Gallery seemingly learned their trade designing the wartime blockhouses defending the white cliffs of Dover. "Brutalism" was the name given to this concrete incoherence.

A decade later, a fresh start on the other, eastern, side of Waterloo Bridge brought happier results. The architect Sir Denys Lasdun thought the King's Reach site he was given for the National Theatre "the most magical in London," and he took advantage of it by fronting the complex with cantilevered terraces offering a panoramic view across the gardens of the Embankment to St Paul's. Behind the concrete ramparts are three auditoriums with different theatrical provenances: the Olivier, Greek classical; the proscenium-arched Lyttelton, and the more intimate "Tudor inn yard" of the Cottesloe.

As a topographical entity, the South Bank stops here, at Waterloo Bridge, but the riverside walk now leads on to further cultural attractions, the Tate Modern gallery and the rebuilt Globe Theatre.

The Brutalist influence on the South Bank is plain to see in the concrete complex that includes the Hayward Gallery (far right). The approaches came in for particular criticism – windy decks, bleak bridges, confusing walkways. Some called the style "ad-hocism."

The National Theatre under construction in 1972 (above). Concert halls better suited to smaller ensembles than the Festival Hall added to the South Bank's musical range. The Queen Elizabeth Hall (left) features an organ console that can be lowered out of sight. Modernism took an eccentric step with the first version of the National Film Theatre (right).

QUEEN ELIZABETH HALL, PURCELL ROOM, HAYWARD GALLERY: LCC ARCHITECTS; SIR HUBERT BENNETT, JACK WHITTLE, 1964

A 435-ft. high arch identifies the new Wembley Stadium on the London skyline. Twin domes distinguished its predecessor, shown below under construction in 1923.

# Playing the game

## SPORTS STADIUMS

As London prepares for the 2012 Olympics, a new football stadium has arisen where the city last hosted the Games – Wembley Stadium, in 1948. BBC TV now carries the address of the Olympic venue of 40 years before that – White City, where a mere

It was terrace standing room only for most spectators at the old Wembley (bottom). What seats there were were sandbag tested. The old stadium had 360 toilets; the new one has 2,618. NORMAN FOSTER & PARTNERS

1,500 competitors from just 19 nations took part in the fourth modern Olympiad.

The capital's other venues for international competitions have proved more durable, though subject to continual restructuring. There's Wimbledon (1922) where the world's leading tennis players gather every June, and Twickenham, the home of English rugby since 1907. Twickenham's planners took the unusual step, for the time, of providing a car park where, ever since, spectators have popped corks in their own pre-match warm-up rituals.

And closest to the capital's heart, geographically speaking, if no longer emotionally,

the two great cricket grounds: Lord's, within walking distance of Marble Arch, and the Oval, just across Vauxhall Bridge. Both were built when so much urban acreage was affordable – the Oval on the flood plain of a now forgotten river. Thomas Lord first marked out a cricket pitch even nearer to the centre of town, but lost the site to property developers. It became a garden square bearing the name of a cricket-loving noble, the Duke of Dorset. Lord's next ground proved to be directly in the path of the Regent's Canal, so his Marylebone Cricket Club finally settled in St John's Wood in 1816.

The MCC spread the game around the Empire – teams from former dominions and colonies are still the international opposition at Lord's – and as the MCC became the game's supreme authority, it earned a reputation for traditionalism. But not in architectural terms. Admired additions to the Lord's complex in recent years include a curvaceous, white-skinned Media Centre high above the stands, a futuristic surprise at such a venerable institution.

Keeping an eye on Lord's (above) from the Media Centre (Future Systems, 1999). Paying spectators, too, have improved conditions, in stands by Nicholas Grimshaw & Partners and Michael Hopkins & Partners. The Oval has also undergone major rebuilding recently, but the ancient gasholder (left) nearby remains the feature that identifies it to watchers of TV cricket around the world.

The sturdy stand being built at Arsenal's Highbury Stadium in 1932 (above) served football fans until the 2006 season opened at the new Emirates Stadium (right), named for the club's airline sponsor. Here, in Islington, North London, specialist stadium architects, HOK Sport, designed accommodation for 60,000 spectators in four tiers of seating under a roof that has the area of four football pitches. In the 1920s, Stamford Bridge offered no such cover for Chelsea fans (top).

The first men's tennis championship was played at Wimbledon in 1877. Now, the Centre Court, (above, and under construction in 1922, left) is the game's most respected arena, one of the few to preserve the founding idea of playing on grass – Lawn Tennis. Wimbledon Fortnight begins with qualifying matches on 16 courts, whittling down to finals played on Centre Court and the No. 1 Court constructed (right) in 1995.

# Desk jobs

## OFFICES

As manufacturing moved away, pen-pushing and paper-chasing became the city's principal activities. By 1912, the Underground and bus services were unloading 250,000 office workers into the City and central London each morning – a workforce that contained a distinctive new element: educated young women for whom teaching and nursing had previously been just about the only respectable employment options. Their clattering typewriters now set the rhythms of London labour.

White-collar numbers grew and grew, all through the 20th century. Rows of Georgian houses became offices for genteel trades such as publishing. Grand hotels beside Trafalgar Square were reinvented and replaced their bedside tables with filing cabinets. The Whitehall bureaucracy spread upriver, along Millbank. Factories decommissioned in Finsbury, close to the City, made way for office blocks. And there was much brutal destruction of old London: Adams's urbane riverside terrace, the Adelphi, was reduced to rubble in pursuit of rentable square footage. In the aftermath of World War II, as bomb sites were filled in, office developers seemed to get ready permission to demolish anything alongside to build a bigger slab.

Until the 1950s there had been a height restriction – 100 ft. (the reach of the firemen's tallest ladders). That became a regulation limiting a building's height to five times its frontage. But pile-boring technology had removed the fear of subsidence into the London clay and ambitions grew taller; the criterion became "on its merits." Developers were given extraordinary freedom to ignore plot ratios and reach upwards. What's more, the promise of a faux-piazza, a token pedestrian precinct, an

The property developers' most conspicuous, and disliked, contribution to the excesses of the Swinging Sixties was Centre Point, straddling a nondescript traffic bottleneck at the eastern end of Oxford Street. Years later, it would be "listed" as meritable enough to deserve preservation. The same architects created the same "honeycomb" effect in pre-cast concrete on a more modest scale at Space House, off nearby Kingsway (above).
RICHARD SEIFERT & PARTNERS

Upper floors canting out over the street
and bands of windows framed in
different colours distinguish Bankside
Studios, a regeneration project in
Southwark where the Tate Modern
gallery has set the pace for local renewal.
CZWG ARCHITECTS, 2004

A view of the river interrupted only by
models of their own projects inspire
architects of the Foster & Partners practice.
Their open-plan double-height studio in
Battersea is topped by five floors of flats.
Lord Foster lives over the shop, as an
Elizabethan employer would have done.

Builders turned their backs on the dirty canal that carried much of Victorian London's supplies. The current Paddington Basin development relishes the situation, featuring the waterfront as the outlook for massive office complexes, for homes, marina facilities, and even floating "business barge" workplaces. (The curve of The Point building, centre, above is dictated by a bend of the canal.) Brunel's railway station is crucial to the project: it houses the Heathrow Express terminal – putting the airport just 15 minutes away – and there are air rights over a rambling old train yard to exploit. Since 1996, an area the size of Soho has been undergoing one of Europe's largest multi-use regenerations.
MASTERPLAN: TERRY FARRELL & PARTNERS

eased traffic flow, produced tax inducements and subsidies – and a blind eye to the aesthetics of the structure. The lumpish Bowater House (1958) has a hole through it to allow entrance to Hyde Park. Centre Point (1967), confusing the topography of St Giles Circus, represented speculation at its most spoiling. Its 35 floors stood empty for nearly a decade.

In the 1950s, such developments were adding as much as 4 million sq. ft. a year to London's office space. Margaret Thatcher's "enterprise culture" of the 1980s raised the stakes again. The City's financial sector was booming, and bursting out of its stockade – while nearby the disused Docklands still lay desolate. Enticed by subsidies from public funds and freedom from planning controls, developers laid plans for 10 million sq. ft. of new office space at Canary Wharf. Intimidated by this competition, the Corporation of the City of London eased its own planning restrictions, speedily giving permission for redevelopment on more than 100 sites. As a result, London gained some exciting, breakthrough architecture, most distinctively the Swiss Re Headquarters – "the Gherkin".

Shell-Mex House advertises "offices to let" shortly after its Art Deco remodelling; its carcass was the huge Cecil Hotel of 1886, stretching back to The Strand. The clockface on the riverside frontage, even larger than nearby Big Ben's, was, predictably, nicknamed Big Benzene.
MESSRS JOSEPH, 1931

The New Adelphi office building's Art Deco detailing might be more respected if it were not for nostalgic recollections of its predecessor on the site near the Strand. Nearly all the last fragments of the Adam brothers' urbane Adelphi Terrace, regarded as Georgian London's most elegant riverside composition, made way for it.
COLLCUTT & HAMP, 1938

At the end of the 1950s, Londoners braced themselves for a Manhattan-style encroachment on the skyline as the Millbank Tower grew and grew (right). They were reassured to learn that its supporting pilings sunk to 98 ft. in the suspect London clay, and were relieved to see curves and unexpected angles in the concrete and steel form. At 394 ft., the Millbank Tower was only briefly London's tallest building.
RONALD WARD & PARTNERS, 1963

American architects drew up the original master plan for the Canary Wharf regeneration, and designed the building that symbolizes it all, 1 Canada Square. It is built of 27,000 tons of steel – 370,000 sq. ft. of it in the cladding. Its 50 floors are approached through a lobby lined in Italian and Guatemalan marble. The 770-ft. tower quickly lost the title of Europe's tallest skyscraper – beaten by the MesseTurm in Frankfurt, London's rival to be the continent's financial centre.

CESAR PELLI & ASSOCIATES ARCHITECTS, 1990

The wheel was put together on pontoons in the Thames. It took a week to raise it to the vertical, not without hitches, as oil-rig methodology was given an unlikely application.

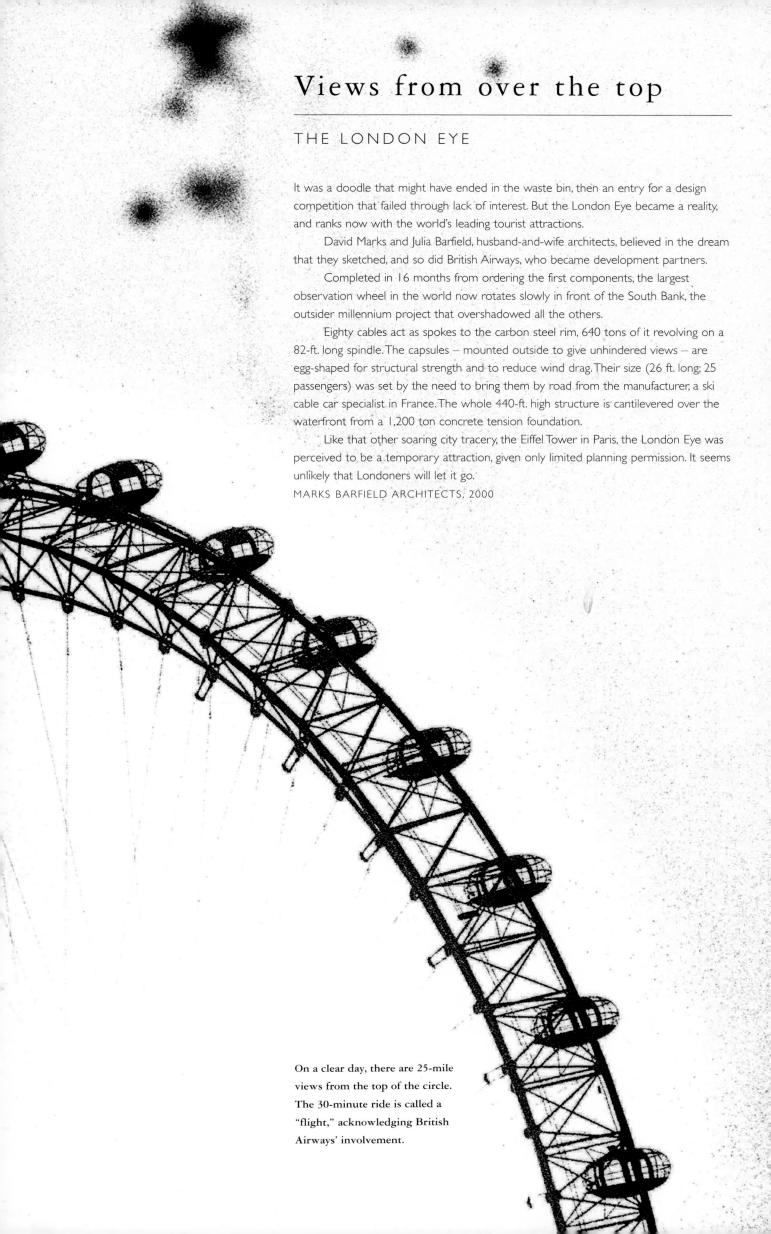

# Views from over the top

## THE LONDON EYE

It was a doodle that might have ended in the waste bin, then an entry for a design competition that failed through lack of interest. But the London Eye became a reality, and ranks now with the world's leading tourist attractions.

David Marks and Julia Barfield, husband-and-wife architects, believed in the dream that they sketched, and so did British Airways, who became development partners.

Completed in 16 months from ordering the first components, the largest observation wheel in the world now rotates slowly in front of the South Bank, the outsider millennium project that overshadowed all the others.

Eighty cables act as spokes to the carbon steel rim, 640 tons of it revolving on a 82-ft. long spindle. The capsules — mounted outside to give unhindered views — are egg-shaped for structural strength and to reduce wind drag. Their size (26 ft. long; 25 passengers) was set by the need to bring them by road from the manufacturer, a ski cable car specialist in France. The whole 440-ft. high structure is cantilevered over the waterfront from a 1,200 ton concrete tension foundation.

Like that other soaring city tracery, the Eiffel Tower in Paris, the London Eye was perceived to be a temporary attraction, given only limited planning permission. It seems unlikely that Londoners will let it go.

MARKS BARFIELD ARCHITECTS, 2000

On a clear day, there are 25-mile views from the top of the circle. The 30-minute ride is called a "flight," acknowledging British Airways' involvement.

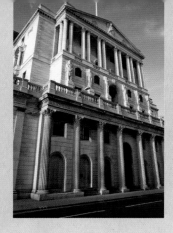

# Circling the square mile

## THE CITY

Despite its venerable customs and inbred self-interest, the City of London has been remarkably adaptable. The "square mile" of financial institutions that grew where the Romans made landfall in England, the ancient heart of the metropolis that still hears the bells of Wren's churches, is, in fact, the capital's chameleon quarter.

It has taken some beatings in its time. Queen Boudicca reduced it to ashes in AD 61. In 1665, a quarter of its population fell to the Plague. A year later, the Great Fire razed two-thirds of it. The Luftwaffe wrought devastation in World War II. And beyond these Acts of God and Reichsmarshal Goering, self-inflicted attrition has constantly changed its appearance. It has been estimated that 80 per cent of the City's fabric was replaced in the second half of the 19th century; half its office space was rebuilt in the decade around 1990 as new working practices forced reconfiguration.

On the guidebook maps, the City's anchoring landmarks are St Paul's Cathedral, the Guildhall, and the Bank of England. All three are rebuilds. Wren's cathedral took the place of one considered to be a wonder of Europe when it was lost in the Great Fire. Only the walls of the medieval Guildhall, the City's administrative headquarters, survived the Fire. Wren reroofed it. A later roof collapsed in the flames of the Blitz, leading to three decades of restoration. The Bank

The NatWest Tower and its slab-sided
neighbours overlook yet another City
clearance. The broader picture below
shows Sir Christopher Wren's church
steeples still poking above the business
boxes. In the shadows at their bases,
medieval alleyways continue to remind
of past communities who worked, and
lived, in "the square mile."

City merchants and traders first made their deals on the street. Then "exchanges" were built for them, still with open trading areas. Not until 1883 did Sir William Tite's Royal Exchange, the third on the site, gain covering for its courtyard – seen here after post-World War II restoration (left).

Rebuilding the Bank of England (right) occupied the entire period between the two world wars. To this day, purists mourn the loss of the gracious banking halls built by Sir John Soane at the turn of the 19th century, and denounce Sir Herbert Baker's lumpish replacement, overlooking the fact that he was required to provide three times more workspace. In 1931, when the work was in progress, Threadneedle Street hoardings came down so that passers-by could see the massive new bronze doors (below left).

From the street, the Corinthian columns of the Royal Exchange have a grander air than this corner of the Bank, to the left in the 1910 photograph below. Flags at half-mast announce the death of Edward VII.

has been on its present site since 1734. Sir John Soane enlarged it behind a security wall which still encloses the rebuild of the 1930s.

The City was a rounded community of residences and workplaces until well into the 19th century. Merchants and private bankers still lived "over the shop," devoting the ground floors of their mansions to business; the tradespeople to serve them – the butchers and bakers and candle makers –occupied meaner homes in the maze of ancient streets and alleys.

But as the City grew to be the world's financial centre, as prosperity flooded through its port, timeless laws of land valuation drove out the citizens to make way for commerce – a customs house and a stock exchange, banks to finance world-wide

When the City closed its ledgers and booted-up computers, when trading with Tokyo became as instant as a handshake, even recent premises were made obsolete. What came down, complexes of cubicles, was replaced by open spaces whose floors housed the lifeline cabling, with work stations set around atriums air-conditioned to cool hustlers and their hard-drives. The Lloyd's of London building took a revolutionary approach to the new ways of working, flaunting the hi-tech in a transparent casing with all its mechanics on show. But the Lutine Bell that formerly advised Lloyd's insurers of good news and bad symbolically survives. RICHARD ROGERS PARTNERSHIP, 1986

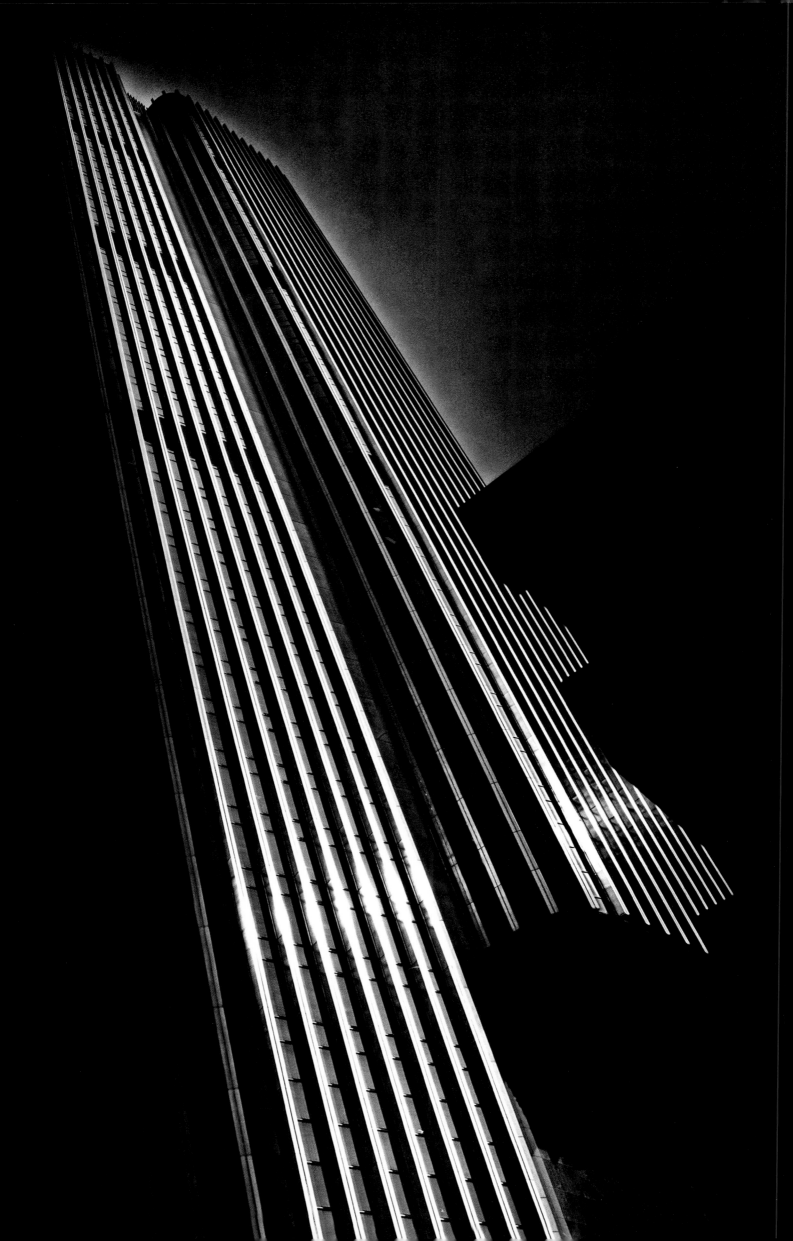

Briefly Britain's tallest building, the National Westminster Tower, now Tower 42 (left) had a long and controversial gestation. Conservationists rallied to protect meritable buildings it would displace, it fell foul of 1960s restrictions on new office development, and traditionalists thought it just too tall – a concern that was to haunt it later when an IRA terrorist attack on the City raised the issue of its vulnerability. However, 20 years after the first proposals, the stainless steel and black glass NatWest Tower opened its doors – an immediate City landmark. But delays and design resubmissions meant that each of its 52 floors cost well over £1 million. RICHARD SEIFERT & PARTNERS, 1980.

The tall and shapely Swiss Re Headquarters (below and right) was, for London, a critical stage in rethinking the practicalities and responsibilities of office environments. Air conditioning is used minimally: dense garden plantings are part of the workspace, re-oxygenating the air – and the windows actually open. Aerodynamic shaping reduces downdraughts in the surrounding pedestrian piazza. The "Gherkin" is London's "first ecological tall building." FOSTER & PARTNERS, 2004

trading, halls for convivial dealing in coal and corn, salerooms for auctioning tea and spices, and insurance companies to reassure the whole whirligig. They all needed a presence close to the action, and as powerful-looking as possible.

The status symbolism of great heights was discouraged in London; even now, the City rarely reaches for the sky in the Manhattan manner. Architects made corporate statements in various authoritative and plutocratic styles – Palladian, Grecian, Baroque, Venetian. And as street-widening was rarely an option, making it difficult for the observer to step back and admire overall appearances, they highlighted surface materials such as polished and coloured stone, and put the power displays inside, in richly detailed and lofty atriums.

Such stylistic conceits are still in play in the latest City regeneration, at the "inside-out" Lloyd's Building with its towering open interior; at the Swiss Re company's "Gherkin" whose shapely surface draws the eye with spirals of glazing. These are among architectural adventures that have helped the City to weather yet another outside attack – Canary Wharf's bid to take over its business.

The Great Court provides breathing space at last in the British Museum, long overwhelmed by artefacts and visitors. The "drum" of the old Reading Room is on the right. The National Gallery (below, c.1870) had to spread outwards into the new Sainsbury Wing.

# Housing a heritage

## MUSEUMS AND GALLERIES

As every enthusiast knows, collections quickly get out of hand. It's no different at state level. The National Gallery began in a Pall Mall townhouse with just 54 pictures; now it takes up the entire north side of Trafalgar Square. The National Portrait Gallery's founding purpose, to display "the most Eminent Persons in British History," was first served by 57 paintings; now it has 10,000 portraits and 500,000 photographs. The new British Library was looking for overflow space even before it was opened in 1998; its right to a copy of every new British publication requires two additional miles of shelving each year.

The British Museum exemplifies the inevitable law of collecting: Artefacts will arrive to fill the space available. The pressure began to mount

The Tate Gallery on Millbank, first funded by Sir Henry Tate, the sugar refiner, has grown over the years through other private benefactions. Tate Modern on Bankside (opposite) was one of the better uses of National Lottery grants. Galleries line the vast turbine hall of this former power station.

Contrasting styles in South Kensington – the Science Museum begun by Sir Richard Allison (1913) and the eminently Victorian Natural History Museum by Alfred Waterhouse (1881). The Science Museum looks a little like Selfridge's: the architect is said to have planned the display spaces on department store principles.

in the 18th century when there were private collections on offer that governments of the day agreed were too important to be broken up. The will of Sir Hans Sloane (Lord of the Manor of Chelsea; thus, Sloane Street and Sloane Square) offered the nation his art, antiquities and natural history collections at a knock-down price; rare manuscripts collected by Earls of Oxford could be acquired. The Lindisfarne Gospels and two copies of the Magna Carta were decaying in storage.

The Duke of Montagu's house on a seven-acre site in Bloomsbury was bought to respectfully contain them. But bequests, purchases and plunder piled up: the Royal Library of 120,000 books, the actor David Garrick's collection of old plays, the

A cathedral-like setting for a dinosaur at the Natural History Museum, where every space and crevice bears Romanesque detail (above).

A more modern approach to display at the National Portrait Gallery (right). The architect Piers Gough sought the effect of joining a party of famous people. Screen walls of glass multiply the hanging space for 20th-century portraits, yet leave the room open.

Rosetta Stone, the Elgin Marbles. The architect Robert Smirke was commissioned to enlarge and enhance as best he could. Finally Montagu House had to go and the classical Greek façade and portico that still grace Great Russell Street emerged to crown Bloomsbury as the intellectual centrepiece of the capital of the world.

But another London borough was making a bid for attention. As Prince Albert had suggested, profits from the Great Exhibition of 1851 were invested in making South Kensington a cultural centre. In 1856, the Science Museum settled here. Nearby, the Natural History Museum absorbed Bloomsbury's collections of fossils and feathers, and what would become the Victoria and Albert began stuffing its "capacious handbag" with sculpture and applied arts.

Back in Bloomsbury, wings and extensions arose over the years. Even the central courtyard was commandeered, to make a study area for students and researchers (1857). Not until 1998 did the museum find room for the calm, interactive social area it sought. Then the new British Library in St Pancras absorbed the book collections, and the Queen Elizabeth II Great Court, an elegant public space refreshed through 3,000 glass roof panels (Foster & Partners, 2003) took the place of bookstacks around the famous Reading Room whose cast-iron dome outdoes both St Paul's and St Peter's.

These national treasure houses were inevitably primed by private philanthropists. Other men with wealth and taste still have their names over their contributions to the city's cultural richness – Tate, Wallace, Soane, Courtauld, Horniman. And in their shadow, dozens of idiosyncratic enthusiasts display their legacies of every imaginable collectable, from toys to bus tickets, playbills to postage stamps.

Sir John Soane Museum in Lincoln's Inn Fields (above) displays London's favourite collection of curiosities. His income as an architect augmented by the fortune of a rich wife, Soane filled his townhouse with treasures and trinkets, then sponsored an Act of Parliament to ensure that his private delights entered the public domain.

The museum first built on the site of the present Victoria and Albert was intended to emphasize the role of science and art in manufacturing (left, top). The building was therefore engineered rather than designed. But the Brompton Boilers, as it was called, was too *outré* for South Kensington; Aston Webb's terracotta building took its place. The metalwork was reassembled as the carcase of the Bethnal Green Museum and the V&A's mementoes of childhood were relocated there (bottom).

The exterior of the British Library – which houses 12 million books – gives few clues to its content (right). Below the bland Euston Road frontage four deep basement floors of bookstacks are approached through generous and richly-detailed public spaces. In 1998 the Queen opened the building that her son, the Prince of Wales, thought resembled "an academy for secret policemen."
SIR COLIN ST JOHN WILSON, 1997

# Spreading the word

## MEDIA CENTRES

**The *Daily Express* was pre-war Fleet Street's flashiest presence, journalistically and architecturally. Curves and setbacks faced in black and chrome preened London's first true commitment to curtain walling (above).**

In 1869, a roll of paper four miles long and twice the width of a broadsheet travelled through a steam-powered press to be printed on both sides at the rate of 1,000 ft. a minute. Fifty-five years after it had been the first newspaper to be printed by a "mechanical apparatus," *The Times* could now truly spread the word, shipping bundles of newspapers around the country through the great new railway termini.

The press for "that volume of Modern History, put forth day by day" thundered in Blackfriars, in Printing House Square, named for the former workshop of the King's printer, the publisher of proclamations and the official *London Gazette*. The rivals who had to catch up were nearby in Fleet Street, long a base for printers, publishers, and pamphleteers. The first newspaper, *The Daily Courant*, had been published from here in 1702. With the rise of the newspaper barons – Northcliffes, Harmsworths, Astors – Fleet Street saw the construction of power buildings.

The strait-laced *Daily Telegraph* built itself a surprisingly modern home (Elcock

**Main picture: a balcony, an alfresco corridor or power, denotes boardroom level at the *Daily Telegraph* building (above).**

and Sutcliffe, 1928); the news agencies Reuters and the Press Association commissioned Sir Edward Lutyens's last commercial building in London (1935). And the upstart Canadian, Max Aitken, later Lord Beaverbrook, was boldest of all. Gleaming black glass sheathed his *Daily Express* building (Sir Owen Williams, 1932); the Enterprise of Empire – a Beaverbrook hobby horse – was depicted in metal relief around London's most extravagant Art Deco reception hall.

In this era, another medium of mass communication arrived, literally out of thin air. Within a decade of its first crackly radio transmissions (1922), the British Broadcasting Company (quickly, "Corporation") was sufficiently sure of itself to take a prime site in the West End, placing the rounded prow of its majestic Broadcasting House a step back from Nash's curvaceous All Souls Church at the top of Regent Street. Very soon, the inner core of 22 sound-proof studios was not enough. The BBC commandeered theatres and concert halls all over London for broadcasts in the innocent days when audience applause was live rather than canned.

The first television transmissions, in 1936, were from Alexandra Palace, on a north London hill. Another former exhibition centre, the White City showground in Shepherd's Bush, made room for the BBC's rambling Television Centre which went on air in 1960. Custom-building for independent television produced two

notable complexes: Terry Farrell's "anti-modern" block in Camden Town for the ill-fated TVAM company, and Richard Rogers' headquarters for Channel 4, a beacon of hi-tech in the gloomy setting of Victorian Victoria.

These bold new frontages all appeared outside the traditional communications village down by Ludgate Circus. Two prestigious news organizations had snubbed that ghetto: serious American money went into the *Time & Life* Building, in Bond Street of all places, where the architects Sir Hugh Casson and Sir Misha Black and the sculptor Henry Moore fulfilled one of post-war London's most extravagant commissions (1952). Less than a mile away, the international business magazine, *The Economist*, built a tower on a plaza, New York-style, in the equally civilised context of St James's (Alison and Peter Smithson, 1964).

Fleet Street was in decline. Much as its population of companionable journalists appreciated its other reputation ("…along that tipling street, Distinguished by the name of Fleet, Where tavern-signs hang thicker far, Than trophies down at Westminster") modernising forces were making nonsense of the location. Premises designed for labour- and machine-intensive rituals were wastefully unsuitable for invisible, digitized, computerized choreographies.

With the electronic processing of words and pictures, there was no longer the need for clattering type-setters to be within copy-boy range of sub-editors; nor photo-engravers to be beside the picture desk; nor plate-makers nearby to trundle the final assemblies to the presses, which could now be satellites all around the country. The whole process could be leaner, more compact, and happen in cheaper locations. Emboldened by Prime Minister Margaret Thatcher's distaste for the union power that aggressively opposed such advances, Rupert Murdoch furtively moved his stable of newspapers to Wapping. Farringdon and Canada Square appeared as masthead addresses, and, unlikeliest of all, the *Daily Mail* declaims from a deconstructed department store off Kensington High Street.

Another media centre flaunting the theatricality of its purpose is the Channel 4 Television headquarters in Victoria, (right), rich with echoes of the architects' thinking at their Lloyd's City building. The mechanics are on show – glass-box lifts, transmitters and aerials – dressed in steel, glass and red ochre.
RICHARD ROGERS PARTNERSHIP, 1994.

TVAM was to be a star-studded commercial channel for London, but its founders' egos clashed and the franchise was lost. Its brazen building in Camden Town survives, a sinuous frontage of corrugated metal and once-bright paint (left).
TERRY FARRELL, 1983

The transmitter tower for the BBC's first TV broadcasts (left) gained range by using the height of Muswell Hill, above studios in Alexandra Palace, north London's rival to the Crystal Palace. The gardens had been landscaped in 1918 by German prisoners of war.

The white Portland stone of Broadcasting House (left, below) was painted in camouflage grey in time for the Blitz, but Luftwaffe bombers found it nevertheless. A monumental lobby inside (above) demonstrated the BBC's early understanding of its own importance as the nation's public service broadcaster.
G. VAL MYERS, 1931

After World War II, the BBC was operating from more than 40 sites in London – none of them suitable for the expected boom in television. Its Television Centre grew on 13 acres of former fairground land at Shepherd's Bush (right).
NORMAN & DAWBARN, 1960